Format for Graphic Designers

Third Edition

BLOOMSBURY VISUAL ARTS
LONDON · NEW YORK · OXFORD · NEW DELHI · SYDNEY

BLOOMSBURY VISUAL ARTS
Bloomsbury Publishing Plc
50 Bedford Square, London, WC1B 3DP, UK
1385 Broadway, New York, NY 10018, USA

BLOOMSBURY, BLOOMSBURY VISUAL ARTS and the Diana logo are trademarks of Bloomsbury Publishing Plc

First edition published in Great Britain in 2005 by AVA Publishing SA
as *Basics Design 01: Format*

Second edition published in Great Britain in 2012 by AVA Publishing SA
as *Basics Design 01: Format, 2nd edition*

This edition published in Great Britain in 2019 by Bloomsbury Visual Arts, an imprint of Bloomsbury Publishing Plc

Copyright © Bloomsbury 2019

Gavin Ambrose and Paul Harris have asserted their rights under the Copyright, Designs and Patents Act, 1988, to be identified as Authors of this work.

For legal purposes the Acknowledgements on p.208 constitute an extension of this copyright page.

All reasonable attempts have been made to trace, clear and credit the copyright holders of the images reproduced in this book. However, if any credits have been inadvertently been omitted, the publisher will endeavour to incorporate future amendments in future editions.

Cover design: Gavin Ambrose
Cover image © 2018 Gingerly Press
See pages 174 and 175 for more work by Gingerly Press

All rights reserved. No part of this publication may be reproduced or transmitted in any form or by any means, electronic or mechanical, including photocopying, recording, or any information storage or retrieval system, without prior permission in writing from the publishers.

Bloomsbury Publishing Plc does not have any control over, or responsibility for, any third-party websites referred to or in this book. All internet addresses given in this book were correct at the time of going to press. The author and publisher regret any inconvenience caused if addresses have changed or sites have ceased to exist, but can accept no responsibility for any such changes.

A catalogue record for this book is available from the British Library.

ISBN: PB: 978-1-4742-9063-0

ePDF: 978-1-4742-9906-0

eBook: 978-1-3500-3182-1

Book design by Gavin Ambrose
Printed and bound in China

To find out more about our authors and books visit www.bloomsbury.com and sign up for our newsletters.

Designed by **Aboud Sodano**, this brochure for a clothing range by **R Newbold** comprises a 42-page section printed in four special colours – black, silver, blue and yellow – rather than the normal process colours. All the images appear as duotones of silver and black. Bound into a hardcover, a die-cut large square creates a uniquely shaped publication.

Contents

Introduction 6

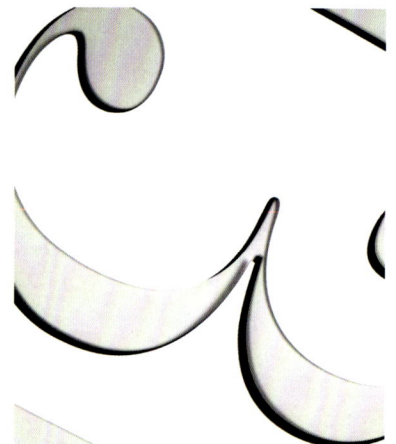

Purpose and narrative 10

Containment and protection 12
   Slipcases 14
   Boxes 16
   Bags 20
   Packaging 24
Storytelling 28
   Typographic 'stories' 30

Context 32

Form follows function 34
   Reveals and discovery 38
   Order 40
   Randomness 43
Shape and form 44
   Dimensionality 46
Online media 48
   Interactivity and
   engagement 50
Converging formats 52
Guidelines 56
Sustainability 64
   Risograph 64
Appropriating technology 66
   Adding value and
   collectability 68

Printed media 71

Standard sizes 72
   ISO and US paper sizes 74
Stocks 78
Imposition and multiple stocks 80
   The value of planning 80
Book as sculpture 84
   Exquisite corpse 85
   Extensions of the book 90
Scale 92
Newspapers 94
   Online trends 94
   Appropriation of format 94
   Denotation and
   connotations 96
Magazines 98
Posters 102
Poster wraps 106
Animation 110

Folding	112	Binding	144	Print and finish	171
Maquettes and printer's dummies	114	Types of binding	146	Printing	172
Folding examples	116	Connotations of binding styles	147	Letterpress	172
Different types of fold	118	Common binding techniques	148	Lino	176
The basic concertina	123	Layflat binding	149	Screen-printing	178
Variations on 'self-covers'	126	Z-binds	150	Print finishing	180
Combining techniques	128	Formal binding	152	Filigree	182
French fold	130	Wiro/comb binding	152	Embossing and debossing	182
Gatefolds, throw-outs and fold-outs	132	Canadian and half-Canadian binding	153	Die cut	184
Throw-ups	136	Informal binding	154	Laser etching	187
Bellybands	138	Open binding	154	Kiss cut	189
Endorse fold	139	Japanese binding	158	Perforation	190
Folding as identity	140	Loose-leaf binding	159	Fore-edge printing	192
Folding for self-containment	142	DIY Binding#1		Lamination and spot UV	194
		Simple thread sewn example	161	Foil	196
		DIY Binding#2		Flock	198
		Japanese thread sewn example	164	Tip-ins	200

Glossary	204
Index	206
Acknowledgements	208

Introduction

Modern design practice has a multitude of tools at its disposal. Layout, typography, colour and images are all critical in differentiating one design from another and relaying information, but an often underrated and underused tool is that of the format itself; the physical presence of the piece.

Format is often overlooked because of its almost exclusively utilitarian nature. This, and the existence of many generic formats, means that format is something that many designers do not realise they are thinking about. The format of a piece of design provides a physical point of contact with the user that affects how we receive both printed and online communication.

We are familiar with a wide range of formats, mainly for ergonomic reasons: a poster needs to be large enough to be read from a distance; a stamp needs to be small enough to fit on an envelope; a book needs to be large enough for text to print at a readable size, but small enough to be held comfortably in the hand. Although printed matter is often predisposed to be of a certain size, shape, extent and weight, designers often use format to vary these and add an extra dimension to their work.

This is the third edition of this book, originally published in 2005 under the title of 'Basics Design: Format'. In revisiting the work contained in this book, it is apparent that the world has changed a lot in that time. We have become more digitally focused and format changes are reflective of this. We now consume more news digitally, e-commerce has become ever more prevalent, and websites, rather than being an 'add-on' or after-thought, are often the basis of a design.

Research Studios used a subtle but effective die cut for this brochure for the **Issey Miyake** store in Tribeca, New York. Artists, musicians and designers were commissioned to show pieces alongside the branded goods within the store, and this juxtaposition is maintained in the brochure's design; this has a central die cut that gives two 'U' shapes either side of the spine. These provide a physical separation by creating a small book within the pages of the larger one so that readers can flip through either section independently. The work was protected by an embossed outer sleeve (above).

Arguably, there is now less opportunity to produce lavish items of print – but the resurgence of vinyl records, with all the associated packaging and merchandise is testament to the fact that consumers still want to 'possess' and own printed items.

The democratisation of technology has conversely opened up the possibilities of small-scale manufacture and print to the contemporary designer. Designers can now print one-offs, produce work with individual covers and content, and in many cases we are seeing design agencies making their own products. These possibilities are potentially going to influence the next generation of graphic designers, who will have the ability to be more experimental and entrepreneurial in their design outputs.

New North Press used a combination of traditional letterpress printing and high-end advanced model making to produce a font (below) that celebrates technology while honouring design routes in older forms of printing.

This combination of technologies and media is reflective of the convergence of design.

In revisiting this book, it was clear that there is still a desire for a return to craft and the tactile nature of design. It was also clear that the basic tenets of design haven't changed, and – if anything – are now more important than ever. This new edition celebrates this sense of craft, revisiting some of the basic things we can do as designers, and includes two new sections on folding ^{page 112} (the basic premise of dividing space and in turn information) and binding ^{page 144} which celebrates the art of making.

While design is seeing many advances in technology and integration of media, there remains a healthy interest and even resurgence in craft. The art of making can help to foster skills in all areas of design. Letterpress typography, (above) is a clear example of this. The art of setting letters by hand can teach the fundamental skills of typography, even if its commercial use is now limited.

> 'To design is to communicate clearly by whatever means you can control or master.'
>
> Milton Glaser

'Design is a plan for arranging elements in such a way as best to accomplish a particular purpose.'

Charles Eames

Chapter 1
Purpose and narrative

When selecting an appropriate format for a design, there are two distinct parts of the design that need to be considered. Firstly, there is its 'purpose'. What is it for? Secondly, there is its meaning or 'narrative'.

All designs need to address these two distinct facets with equal vigour. As a designer, you need to consider the purpose that your design will serve, and any special considerations this will entail. Does the design need to protect something fragile? Are there restrictions placed on production costs? Are there specific reasons why certain substrates and materials might not be appropriate?

But design is also about telling a story. It is about conveying information or values about a product or service. Choice of format can have an impact on this, affecting how we perceive a brand or design. This 'narrative' of a design is expressed through both the shape, scale and design but also through material choices and textures. Having a clear purpose and narrative will help you design with a specific vision and intention.

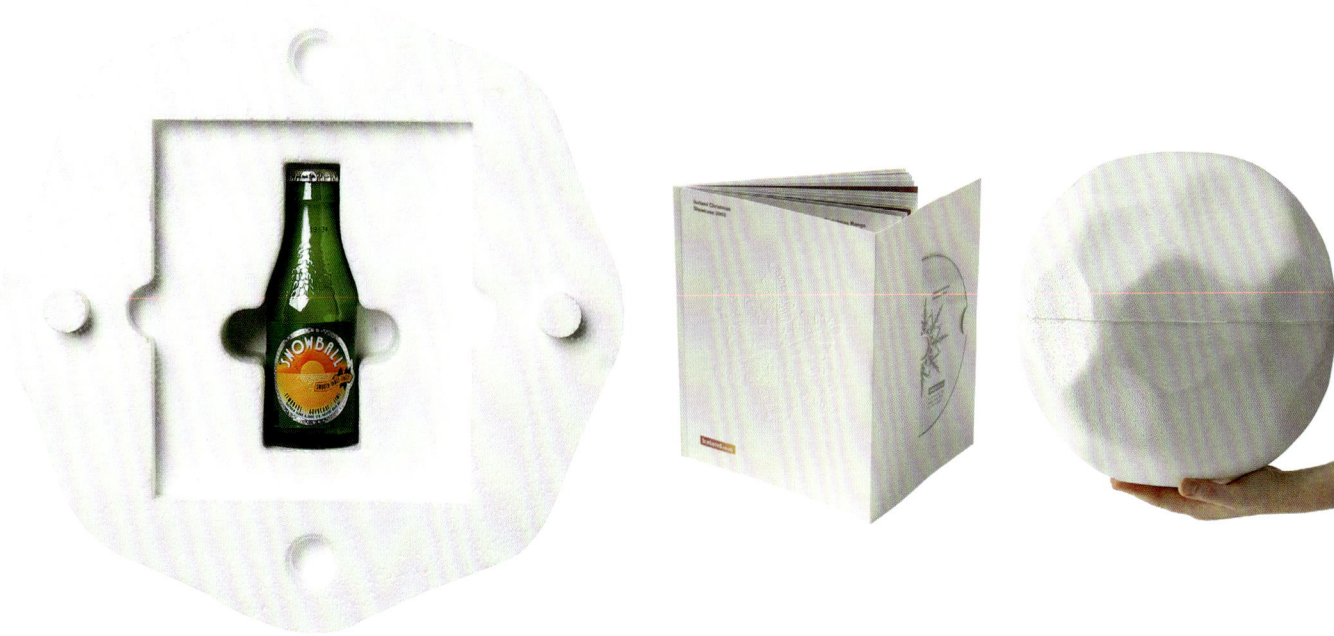

Containment and protection

A major consideration in design is the containment and protection of the object or function being created. This can be in the form of a simple book, where the pages are bound (contained) in an outer cover (protection), or more elaborate and intricate designs. All designs have one thing in common though; the need to tell a story. A design inherently has a sense of narrative; as the pages of a book turn, or a piece of packaging 'reveals' itself, the design 'reveals' a sense of story and communication.

Iris Associates created something extraordinary for UK food retailer **Iceland** in this direct mailer to journalists. Not happy to merely produce a brochure to advertise their Christmas food range, the studio packaged the contents of the mailer in a polystyrene snowball. The campaign received extensive coverage in both consumer and design media.

Entitled 'turn to', this poster/brochure for **Doric**, a road-sign manufacturer, instructs readers on how to unfold the product. Completion of each instruction reveals another page, gatefold or throw-up, reflecting the nature of the signage business. Design agency **Roundel** make explicit use of the structure of a book and the way it reveals content as the user interacts with it. The simple hierarchy uses a single typeface with a reduced number of weights and sizes to simply set out a narrative, encouraging interaction.

Slipcases

A slipcase is generally a box structure made from a hard and durable substrate to contain and protect a book, or to group several books together in one package. A slipcase also adds another element to the presentation of the product. It is open at one end so that the book's spine is visible and will naturally have slightly bigger dimensions than the items it is to contain, which are designed to fit snugly inside.

The slipcase can also be effectively used to contain a series of related or disparate elements within a single binding, adding a sense of value and collectability.

The slipcase can either be a dramatic design element, as in the example on this page by **Form Design**, featuring photographs by Bob Gruen of seminal punk band, **The Clash**. Alternatively, it can be a more subtle intervention, as in the packaging of several books together as one product. This project (opposite) for **Canongate Books** by **Pentagram** partner Angus Hyland, contains copies of the Old Testament and the New Testament, in a slipcase reflective of the book designs it contains.

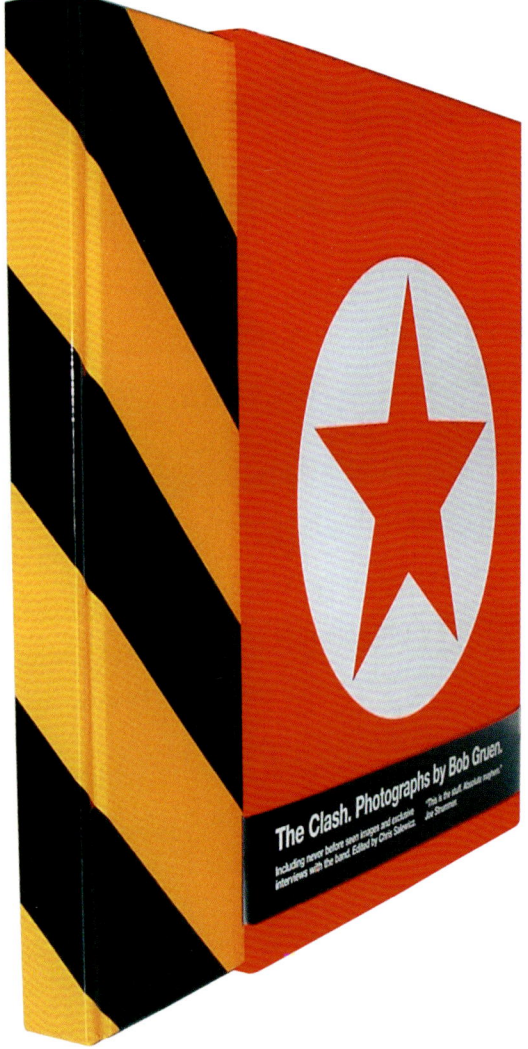

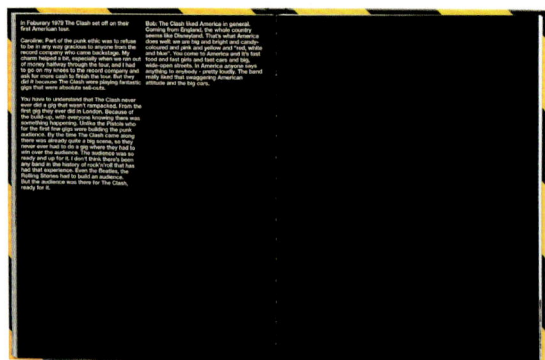

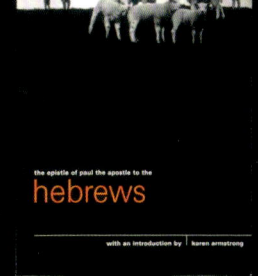

Boxes

A box as a device for containing a set of materials has a different set of considerations and implications to a book. It is arguably less structured, as the contents are generally loose and therefore can be rearranged. A box, however, still retains a formal quality to it, being rooted in photographic archival practice (the box protects the contents from light as much as physical damage). The covering of the box is usually a buckram cloth, but can, of course, be designed and re-appropriated to suit any design. The box itself can also become an integral part of the design, as in the example shown on this page where the box inners are also printed on.

A box also presents a sense of ritual and exploration, as the user unveils the contents – a way of presenting printed materials in a way more aligned with how we as consumers interact with packaging and consumer goods. Related or disparate items and designs can be equally accommodated in this device, as the example on this page shows, with photographic and line art 'pages' being unified through format.

Below is **Woven**, a trend-forecast book for the fashion and textile industry designed by **MadeThought**. This edition is a loose-leaf binder contained in a cloth-covered box, which allows the files to be contained, but also allows for them to be altered, changed or added to in the future.

A box can add to the collectability of books, records and products. As art director for publishing house Foruli, **Andy Vella** has pushed the boundaries of the 'book' format. His recent work for **Elektra Records** has resulted in the creation of lavishly and thoughtfully produced issues, forming a collectable and engaging series of works.

Chapter 1 / Purpose and narrative

An annual report (opposite), art directed by prominent British architect **David Chipperfield** and designed by **John Morgan** studio, for professional lighting company **Zumtobel Group.** The books, akin to a piece of art in their own right, are carefully designed and printed – exploring the subtleties of white on white and layerings of diffused textures. The detailing of the box adds a level of care and perceived value to the product.

This print collateral (right) for **The Citigroup Private Bank Australian Photographic Prize** by **The Collective** design agency, uses a combination of stocks and printing techniques to create a subtle, understated effect. The outer containers, boxes and envelopes use a silver stock, that has typography applied as a debossed silver foil. This silver on silver process creates a strong identity and sense of modern simplicity. The accompanying photographic images are printed CMYK on to a smooth, high white stock.

Shown above is a bag, created as part of a campaign by design agency **SEA**, for **Monotype**, celebrating 100 years of Edward Johnston's typeface used across the London Underground system. To mark the centenary, a visual language and suite of materials was created, including posters and packaging (shown on page 25 of this book).

In contrast to the formality of boxes and slipcases, the bag is arguably a more informal way of collecting and compiling printed material. Many bags are also inherently more sustainably friendly, often using recycled materials and allowing for reuse after their initial intended use has expired.

Shown opposite is a selection of printed tote bags by **Progress Packaging**. They feature the work of various design agencies, and exemplify the attraction of the utilitarian tote bag. The bags were exhibited at the **SEA** gallery in London.

 Airside
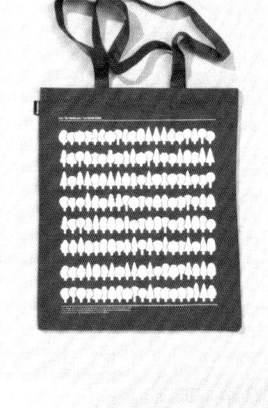 BB/Saunders
 Browns

 Design Project
 Made Thought
 Multi-storey

 NB Studio
 Non Format
 ODD

 Progress
 Supermundane
 The Designers Republic

Designed by **SAS** for an exhibition entitled 'Inside Cover' for **Making Space Publishers**, this catalogue challenges the traditional brochure format. Rather than being bound into a coherent whole, the pages are collated into a bag that closes with press studs. The titles of the posters are printed on the outside fold edge so that they can be easily identified when stacked. Each poster features an exhibit of a participating designer or artist.

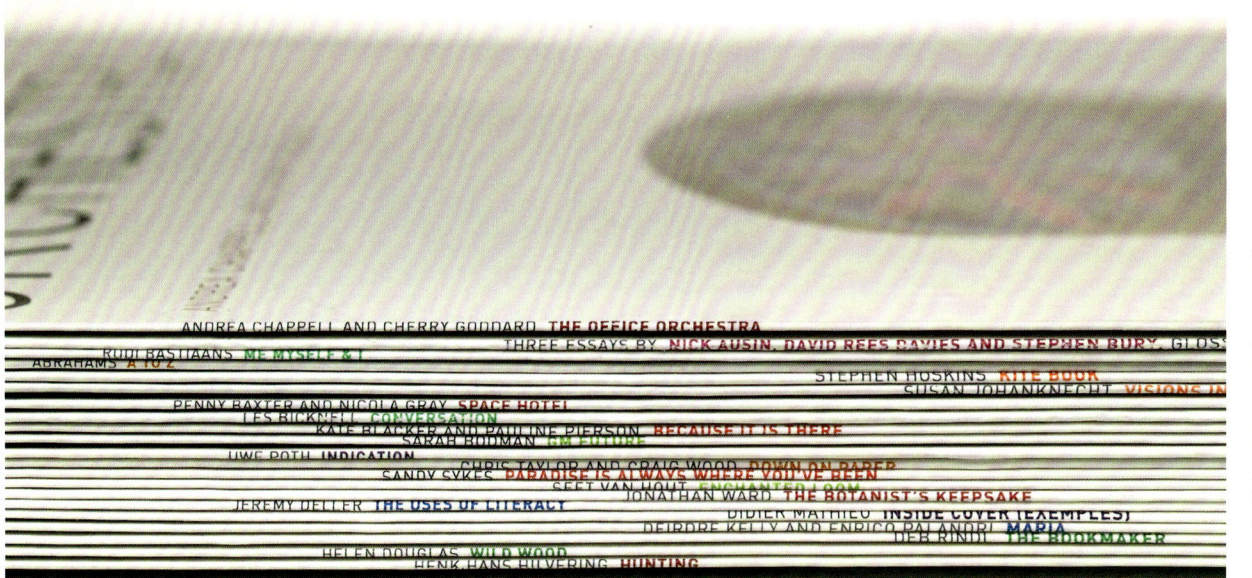

Packaging

All design – whether editorial or product – has a sense of ritual in the way a user interacts with it. This is arguably most explicit in packaging design. Any piece of packaging design contains the two main elements discussed in this chapter; 'purpose' and 'narrative'. It has a function, most obviously to protect the product in transit and through the purchase cycle, but it also tells a story – it has a narrative.

We have a very human interaction with packaging: it connects us emotionally with the things we consume, and the things that we give as gifts to others. **Distil Studio** tapped into this very direct human interaction in their re-branding of **Springs' Smokery**. Taking the charcoal embers of oak logs from their fifty-year old smoking kilns, the design agency created a series of emotive marks and textures to represent the qualities of the product.

This packaging forms part of a campaign by design agency **SEA**, for **Monotype**, celebrating 100 years of Edward Johnston's typeface used across the London Underground system. The packaging acts as an extension of values of the typeface building on the modernist values and confident visual language of the typeface.

Packaging, as with all forms of design needs a focus. Any given product or service can have multiple 'stories' or propositions and one of the roles of the designer is to decide which one to focus on. This branding for **The Cold Pressed Juicery** by **BIA (Build In Amsterdam)** exemplifies this clarity of vision. The geometric graphic pattern represents fruit being cut and is applied to all packaging, stationery and is interpreted into the in-store design. The dividing shapes help to distinguish a clear hierarchy of information, helping to position the brand with authority and clarity of vision.

'Packaging serves many functions. Its design has the ability to shape your subconscious vision of the purpose, quality and benefit of the product'

Herbert Meyers and Richard Gerstman

Storytelling

Many formats offer a fixed narrative. Books, for instance, have a start, a middle and an end, and these are usually fixed in order by binding. Designers can use this intrinsic order and pace to convey stories and narratives – arguably the key to graphic design.

The range of tools available to a designer is relatively small and basic, but having a good understanding of them takes time to master. Clarity of typographic hierarchy and a clear vision of the flow of spreads helps to create a harmonious design. Many designs are based on a grid, in order to instill a sense of order and accuracy. But a grid is only a guide, and design composition comes as much from intuition and practice as it does from mathematics. Designers need to consider how designs work in isolation, spread by spread, but also how a design works more holistically, as a whole. So-called 'patternicity' is the human tendency to seek order and patterns – in effect, to make sense of what we are seeing. However, good design contains enough diversity to remain interesting, and a designer can control this by adding variations to spreads, for example going from gridded to full bleed, as in the example opposite and below, to add interest and pace.

Planning Unit exploit creative possibilities in this events catalogue (left and opposite) for the **London International Documentary Festival (LIDF)**, produced in association with **UpCreative**. The resulting design makes use of flood colour pages to break up the content.

'The grid is actually quite simple, the formatting of the different types of information is very strict, but we tried to make the positions within the layout as varied and dynamic as possible, this way you get something that has a sense of pace and activity, but has a great deal of consistency and clarity.'

Typographic 'stories'
It is often said that we 'read' text and 'see' an image. In reality, we also see typography as shape, and form and interpret any connotations and associations attached to it. This cultural 'baggage' comes with all typefaces and the selection of font styles used has an impact on how we interpret and read text. As a designer, you need to have a clear intention of what you are expecting the typography to do, and not to simply set type. Having a clear vision and understanding of typographic styles will aid in the clarity and delivery of communication, be it in print, on screen or in the built environment.

Twin magazine is a cloth-bound, hard-backed bi-annual that showcases art, culture and feminist features alongside commissioned fashion photography. Each page tells a story, using contrasting poster typefaces, a consistency of centred text and bold fashion photography.

Twin uses an amalgamation of different formats to present its photographs, giving the magazine pace. Passe-partouts and full-bleed images are used throughout, encouraging readers to focus on each page before continuing onwards with the story.

'Good design is making something intelligible and memorable. Great design is making something memorable and meaningful.'

Dieter Rams

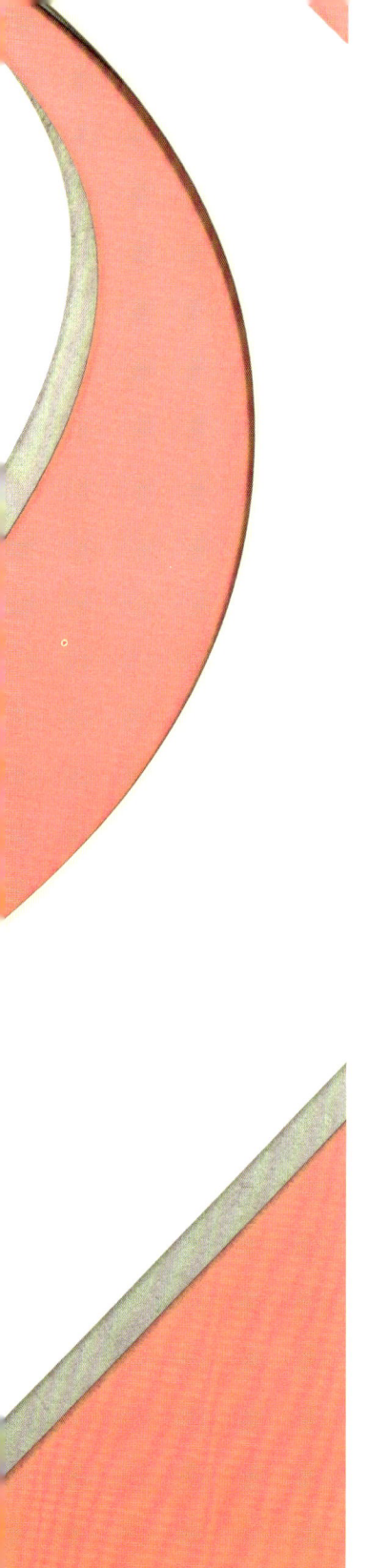

Chapter 2
Context

The context within which we design isn't fixed, and it changes in response to global political, ethical and social issues. The role of the designer has changed in relationship to these concerns, with designers now working across a multitude of platforms and formats, and responding to global trends and concerns such as sustainability and ethical practice.

Technology convergence has resulted in information being viewed by users on multiple platforms and spaces. What once was static (posters on the underground, for example) is now very much active and dynamic. Websites have become populated with film, bringing together two mediums that were once very separate. We have also witnessed an advance in hand-held technology that has changed the way we view content in a fundamental way. Designers working today need to face these contemporary challenges and strive to facilitate meaningful communication across a broader range of devices and platforms.

This chapter looks at some of the contextual concerns surrounding graphic design practice.

Form follows function

It is a commonly held belief that design has two discreet functions – its form and its function. A design's form is its physical manifestation, while its function is what it is trying to communicate. Ultimately, some of the best designs occur when form and function merge seamlessly together, creating a solution that is greater than the sum of its parts.

> 'Form follows function – that has been misunderstood. Form and function should be one, joined in a spiritual union.'
>
> Frank Lloyd Wright

To demonstrate the ability to print on a new high-quality transparent paper, **Radley Yeldar** created this brochure for the paper company McNaughton's product, **Zanders**. The humorous design uses the transparency of the stock to juxtapose an image printed in orange on to photographs by John Edwards that appear on facing pages: by turning the trace-link page, a jelly mould becomes a swimmer's hat (below) and a candle flame becomes a water droplet (opposite).

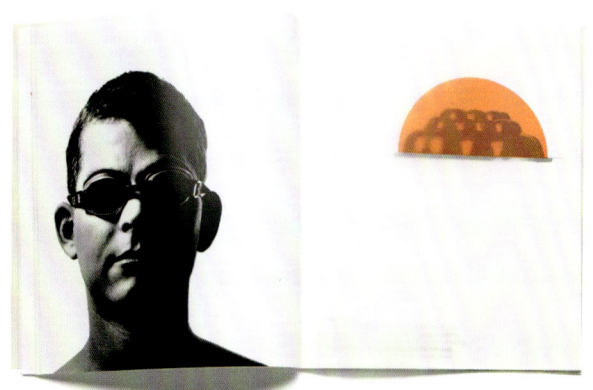

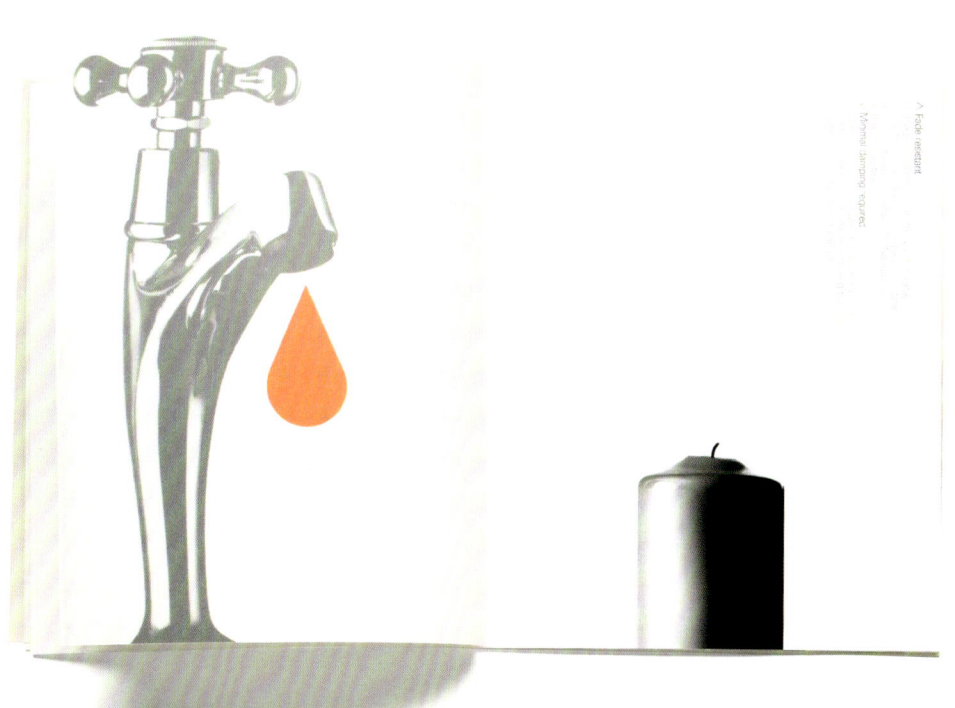

An annual review (opposite) for the **Bailhache Labesse Group** created by **HGVFelton**. The review consists of three different-sized, saddle-stitched publications bound together, all of which cover 'the past', 'the present' and 'the future' of the organisation. All have high-gloss covers with a spot-varnish border and use the subtle cropping of recurrent images to demonstrate the progression of time. The typography reflects the chronology of the brochures, with the past using a 'thin', the present using a 'regular' and the future using a 'bold' version of a single typeface.

Agitprop based this mailer (left) for fashion label **Melt London** on a six-panel concertina fold. To convert it into a mailer, two semi-circles were die cut on the vertical sides of the piece to allow boards to be held in place, front and back, by a rubber band. The binding device is pragmatic; designed to contain a set of images, but it also conveys a story or narrative and a picture of a modern, clean brand with a sense of fun.

Reveals and discovery
Using reveals, or 'punch-throughs' allows a sense of discovery on the part of the user. This control of pace and content can help to form stories and narratives. It can also add a sense of interactivity and order, with certain 'parts' of the information being released at staged intervals.

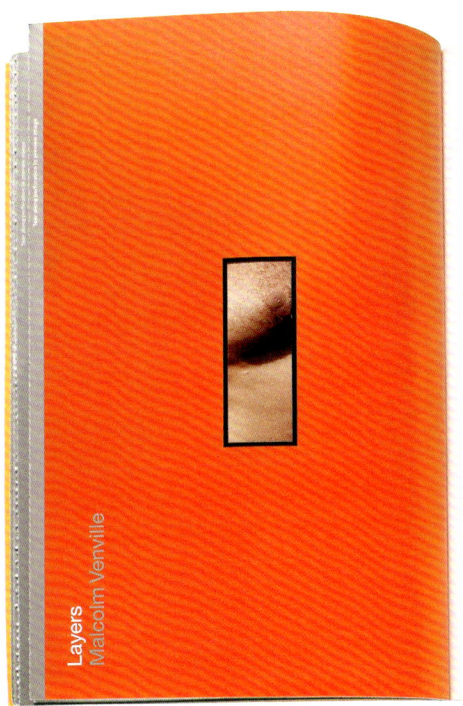
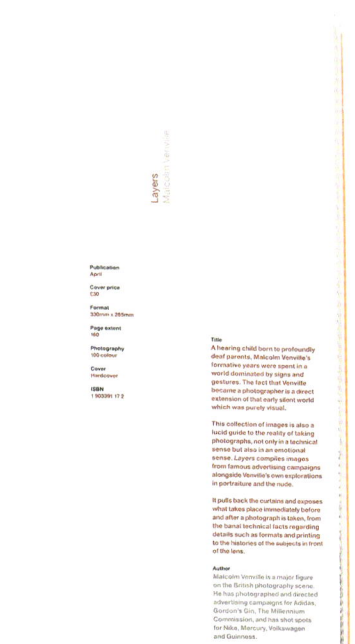

Rose Design created this catalogue (left) for **Westzone Publishing**, a company based in Venice, Italy, as part of an identity campaign to put the company firmly on the publishing map. Pictured is the preview catalogue of its titles, with a die-cut aperture that allows the reader to see through to subsequent pages. This makes a juxtaposition of images, from the harrowing views of Auschwitz to the reportage photography of Malcolm Venville. The French-folded pages are perforated on the outer edge, enabling readers to open them and discover the full 'story' the image has to tell.

Order

Arguably, the role of a graphic designer is, at least in part, to bring order. Arranging, editing and distilling information into a tangible and understandable form is one of the key jobs of a designer.

William Addison Dwiggins, the American type designer and calligrapher, coined the phrase 'graphic design' in 1922, as a means of describing a range of often unrelated tasks that he performed as a newspaper designer, from cutting-out to laying-up, and from drawing to specifying type.

Many contemporary design agencies are rooted in this tradition and have been influenced by the Swiss Design and Modernism of the 1950s onwards.

Canal Building prior to development

Created by **Cartlidge Levene** for the **Canal Building** in Shepherdess Walk, London, this brochure (right) was designed to promote the loft-style development of a formerly derelict building. Made from two sections, one comprises 84 pages printed on a silk stock with commissioned imagery of the surrounding area; the other section is printed on an uncoated stock and contains building plans and other details. The last page of the first section wraps around to form a cover for the whole publication. This piece acts as both a means of clear, ordered communication, utilising the innovative format to divide information, and also as a symbol of the design values of the development.

A classic 1930s industrial property in London N1, Canal Building is being expertly and imaginatively transformed into 74 spacious loft apartments designed by architects Child Graddon Lewis.

Right on the historic Regent's Canal, at 135 Shepherdess Walk, these live/work and residential loft apartments combine waterside tranquillity with easy access to the City and the shops and restaurants of Islington. Close by are the vibrant creative communities of Shoreditch and Clerkenwell.

On five storeys, the apartments have

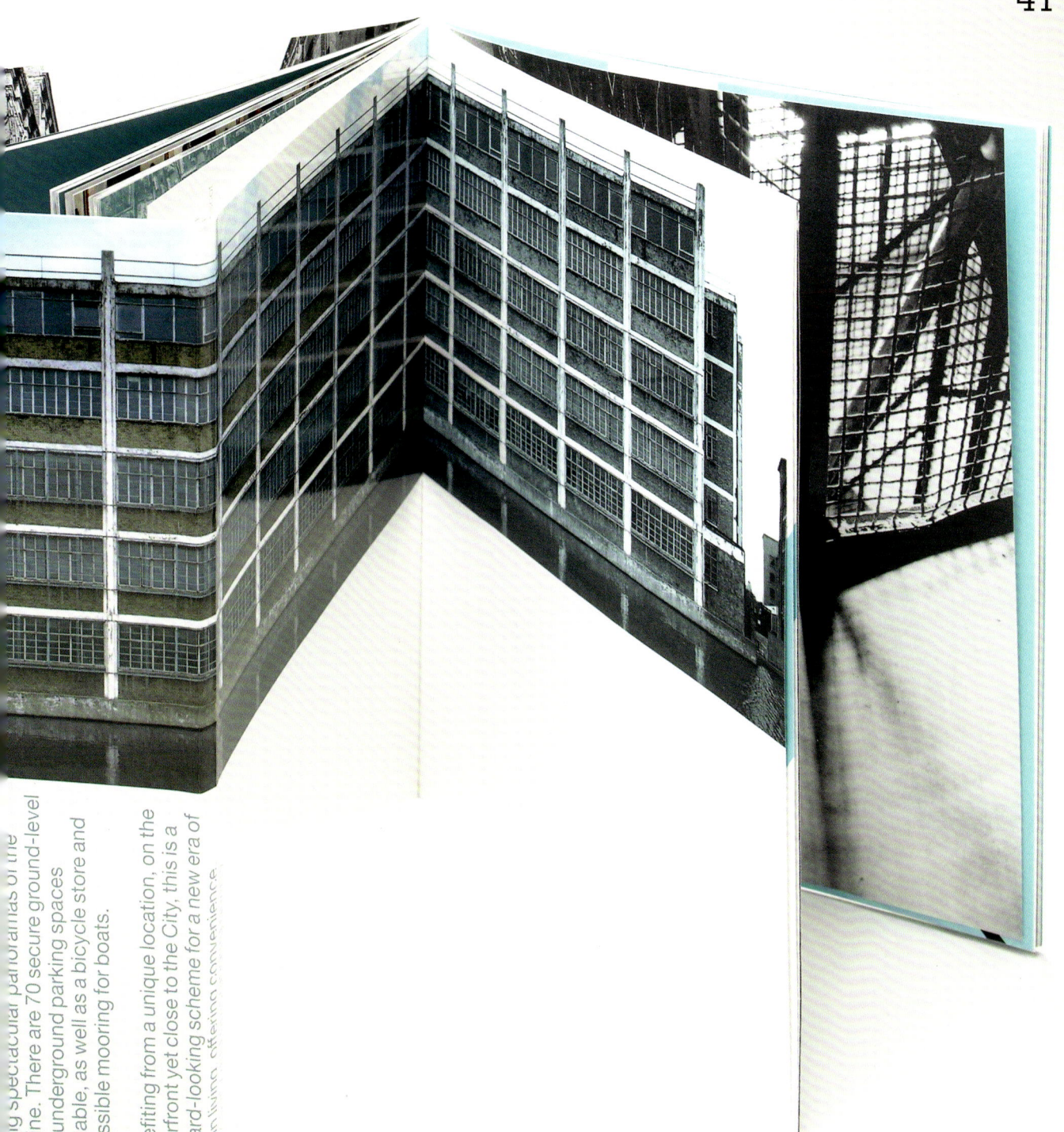

giving spectacular panoramas of the skyline. There are 70 secure ground-level and underground parking spaces available, as well as a bicycle store and a possible mooring for boats.

Benefiting from a unique location, on the waterfront yet close to the City, this is a forward-looking scheme for a new era of urban living, offering convenience

Randomness

Designers often want to control the order in which information is disseminated, and this often involves creating a sense of order. However, there is also value in not trying to control or prescribe this, and in simply letting users 'experience' or create a narrative for themselves instead. This more 'haptic' approach allows for interaction, touch and the possibilities of chance. The unintentional 'pairing' of words and images presents possibilities beyond the conventions of traditional design and has been actively encouraged by designers for centuries including the DADA movement, the Surrealists and the development of assemblage, décollage and the generation of games to encourage the notion of the 'happy accident'.

Randomness as a practice is rooted in a postmodern tradition that rejected the earlier modernist movement values of a single or 'meta-narrative'.

Introducing notions of interactivity makes good communication sense by engaging and including the user in an active way, and has been proven to increase attention and understanding in contrast to more passive communications.

This catalogue, designed by **Aboud Sodano** (opposite) for British fashion designer **Paul Smith**, is based on a children's card game, featuring products and associated name plaques that offer playful randomness.

Shown above is a guide to a new Indichrome printing system for **CTD Capita Digital.** The design by **Hat-trick** is based on the Pantone colour swatch-book and produces more accurate colours than previous digital printing services, These are highlighted in the design by printing the 'names' of various colour hues and intensities in their respective colours.

Shape and form

The shape and form of printed and manufacture of design solutions can be integral to their identity and realisation. The 'shape' of something is a very human quality, and is as concerned with how something 'feels' as much as how something 'looks'.

Changes in technology now mean that as a designer you have the ability to prototype and produce work on a small scale or so-called 'small-batch' runs – be it in print or in three-dimensional form. This democratisation of technology has also enabled the designer to become the manufacturer in many cases, with design studios now regularly producing their own designs and successfully marketing them.

DodeCal is a polyhedra (twelve-sided) calendar, designed and manufactured by design agency **Delivered by Post**. The unique, tactile calendar is honed from a single piece of American Cherry wood and then laser-engraved, rotating the block for each calendar month. The identity and packaging reflect the unique slanted shape of the product.

The design is as much about how it feels as how it looks, creating interesting graphic patterns in the wood while being a celebration of technology, mathematics and craft.

Dimensionality
Increasingly, the role of the graphic designer had moved into roles involving 3D constructions. Adding dimensionality to a design can enable more engaging communications, by encouraging a sense of interaction with the target audience. This can be achieved through innovative technology and approaches to materials, such as those shown opposite. Equally, it can be achieved using tried and tested simple techniques like paper folding, to create a point of difference.

Shown here (right), is a fundraising invite for the **Almeida Theatre** in Islington, London, asking people for a donation in exchange for naming a theatre seat after the donor. The design by **NB Studio** features two die cuts at a right angle to the central creased fold, turning an empty space into a seat and creating the silhouette of a person sitting.

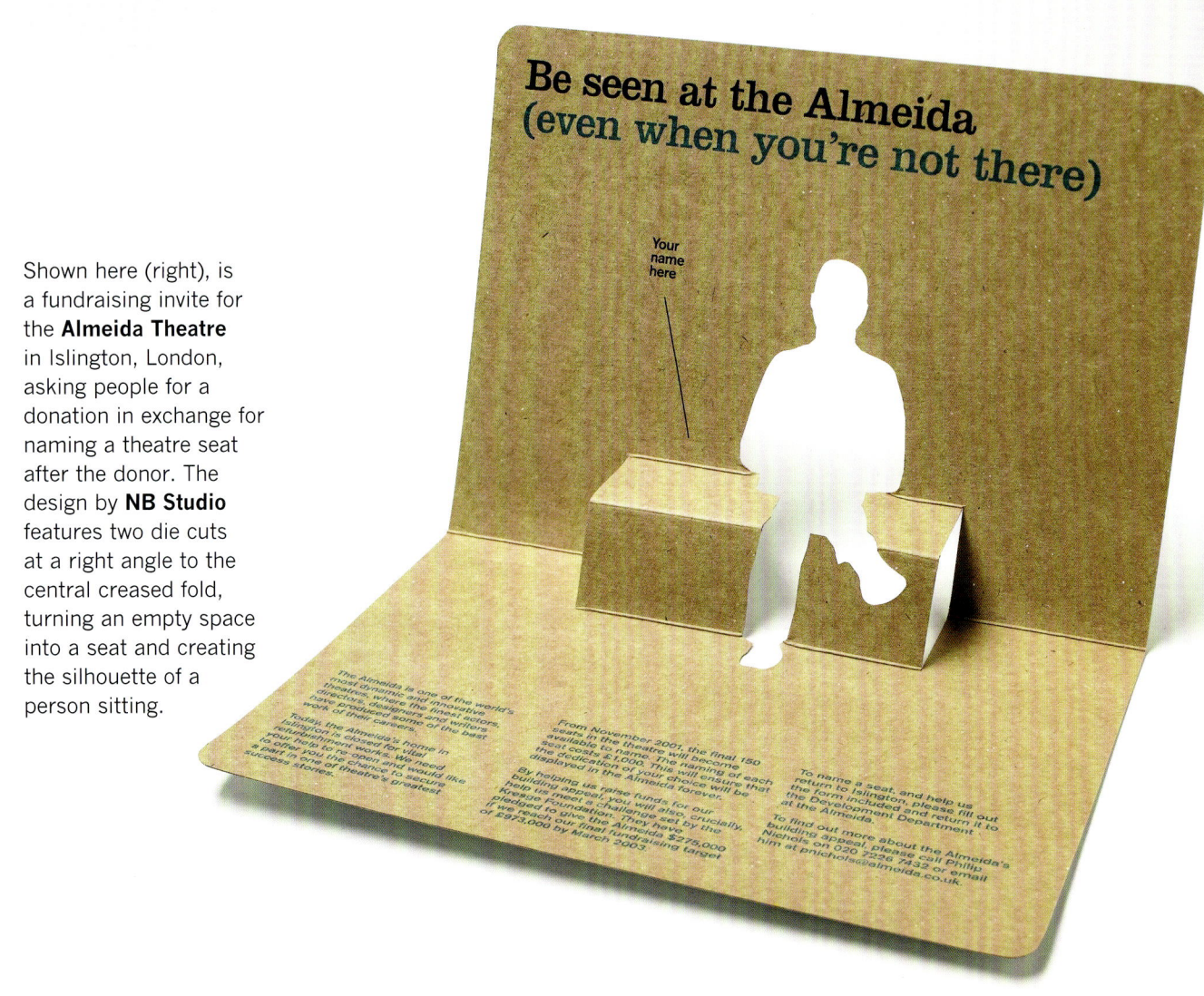

A selection of two- and three-dimensional graphic elements for **'K'** the label of **Karl Lagerfeld**, designed by **Boy Bastiaens**. The designs feature the pixellated portrait pictogram of Karl Lagerfeld, laser cut to create interest and texture. The 'K' emblem was further developed into iconic store furniture.

Online media

The explosion of content on websites is unprecedented. Consumers now access music, watch film footage and browse web pages with new-found freedom. Arguably these forms of media and content are gradually merging as programming moves away from the 'fixed' to the 'fluid'.

Shown below is an image of the now closed **Lust** design studio, that was based in Holland. This early website, created circa 1995, challenged the conventions that were being applied to the format of the web. It used scroll bar devices, usually only found on the bottom and right-hand side extremities of a web page, as a device to create a series of vignettes within which to explore.

Clearly, technology has evolved at an accelerated rate, and with the advances of mobile technology, so has emerged a need (or desire) for content to work seamlessly across multiple platforms. Herein lies the danger of technology being the driver of online design and content, as opposed to traditional design considerations. This shift has, in turn, made the role of branding ever more important. As homogenisation of technology prevails, the role of design to create a point of difference will emerge through confident branding and hierarchical simplicity, as shown opposite.

Designed by **Planning Unit** for **Knoll**, during Clerkenwell Design Week, London in 2011, this iPad 'lookbook' (opposite), demonstrates a confident use of colour and brand in a size-specific format. Shown opposite below is the landing page, an expression of the brand's confidence. The 'virtual' waiting area (shown opposite, above right) leads through to an index page (opposite, top left).

50

Interactivity and engagement

The migration of communication to online platforms, from traditionally print-based formats, brings with it a chance to rethink how content is delivered. Ultimately, platforms will continue to evolve, but the underlying intentions of the designer remain the same; to communicate in an engaging and effective way with a given audience. Arguably, many of the skills of a print designer are transferable to new approaches to delivering content. The considerations of hierarchy, pace, intent, and brand proposition are all equally important in both book and online format. What does, however, undoubtedly change is the way in which this content is presented. Film and moving image provides a visual shorthand for creating greater interactivity and engagement with an audience.

'The Typewriter' (opposite) is a commercial production made by students of the **Film Academy Baden-Wuerttemberg** for the **International Society for Human Rights**. It is an impressive film about freedom of expression which raises awareness of the danger that journalists face when reporting on politically sensitive international issues.

Why not associates decided against industry-standard film equipment to shoot an ident for **Virgin Special Projects**, preferring to use 16 mm instead (left). This film format has its own unique aesthetic that imparts into the subject matter a vibrant grittiness akin to that of a road movie. This was enhanced with lots of post-production, including overlaid type and illustration.

'True interactivity is not about clicking on icons or downloading files, it's about encouraging communication.'

Edwin Schlossberg

Converging formats

As formats converge and become more integrated, the role of the designer arguably becomes more encompassing. A single design may be used or 'rolled-out' over a multitude of different platforms, items and consumer touch points. Any given design has to be adaptable, allowing it to be used over a wide range of media including static and moving items. Depending on the scope of a campaign, these considerations will differ, but generally a design should be thought of with flexibility and growth in mind.

seite zwei – branding & design created this identity and campaign for the 2018 Viennese Modernism exhibition for **WienTourismus** marking the 100th anniversary of the deaths of Gustav Klimt, Egon Schiele, Otto Wagner and Koloman Moser.

The grid system and four distinct key visuals reinterpret the work of Koloman Mosers.

Any campaign needs to contain elements that are adaptable enough to be used over a variety of mediums and product applications. The strong typographic and image design makes the campaign both adaptable and memorable – creating a sense of consistency, while allowing for diversity and surprise in application.

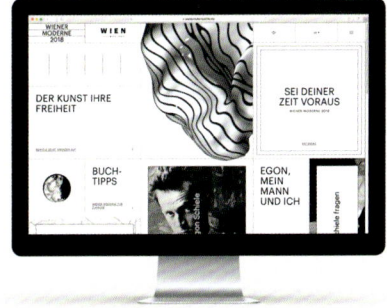

The application of a brand over a wide range of media requires both consistency and the creation of elements that allow for dynamism and playfulness. Any design system shouldn't restrict creativity, but instead should make design decisions easier. Sometimes these decisions are pragmatic, for example the limitations of some printing process will inform the design, as in the case of the tote bag, left, which prints in a single colour.

55

Guidelines

As seen on the previous spreads, the convergence of media and the expansion of the remit of graphic design means that campaigns and brand implementations are often cross-platform, cross-media and even cross-continent. For this reason, the ability to accurately express a brand or product's proposition is often consolidated into a series of values or guides, to ensure the brand is consistently used.

Brand guidelines are primarily aimed at supplying information to partner designers and suppliers. However, they are a useful exercise in testing the viability of a brand – that is to say, does it actually 'work' when applied over a variety of media?

The ability to explain to others how to use a brand is often far more complex than you might at first imagine. It is often as much about telling people what not to do as it is what they can do. A successful set of guidelines will go beyond being simply pragmatic instructions, and should help to convey the energy and values of a brand.

Fact Studio created this identity scheme for **Common Objective**, a platform based business connecting sustainable focussed clients and manufacturers within the fashion industry.

The identity makes explicit use of the idea of connection through colliding images and typographic expression. Shown opposite are spreads from the brand guidelines, that reference how the brand should be used to maintain consistency.

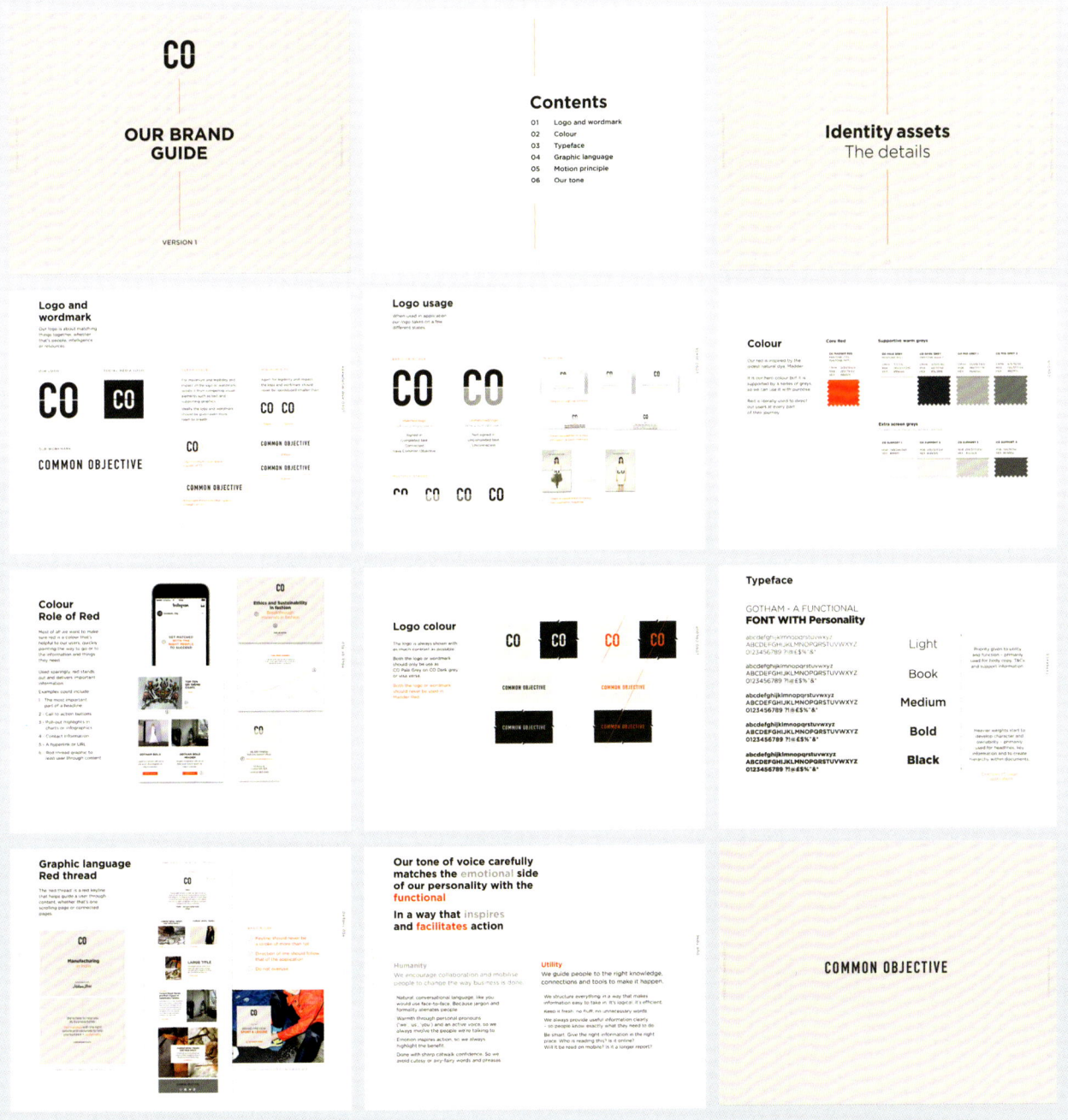

As designs are often implemented by a range of designers in different countries or regions, the need to establish clear and easy to follow guidelines is becoming increasingly important.

Guidelines should serve as a device for enabling creativity and bringing consistency across campaigns and identity schemes.

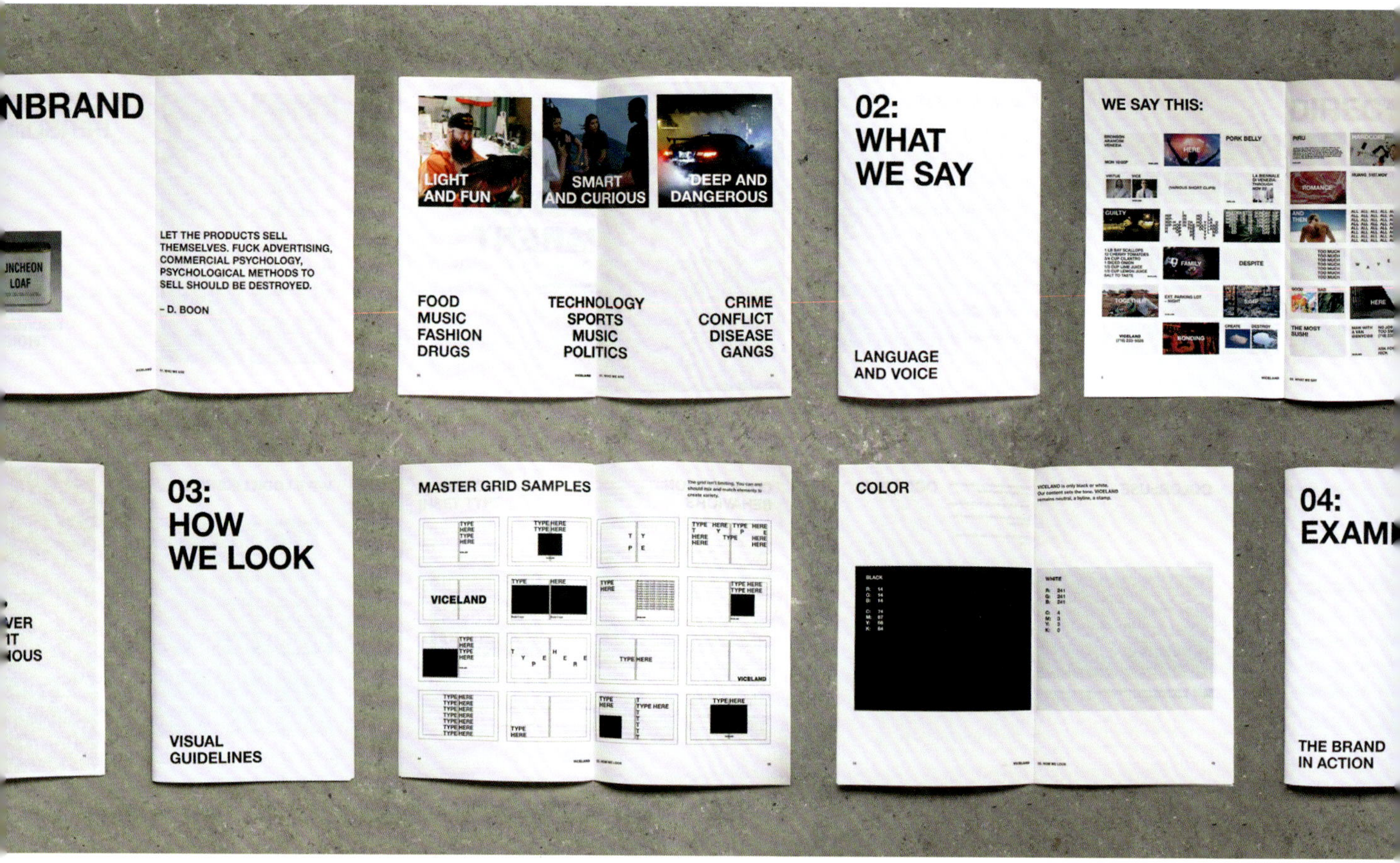

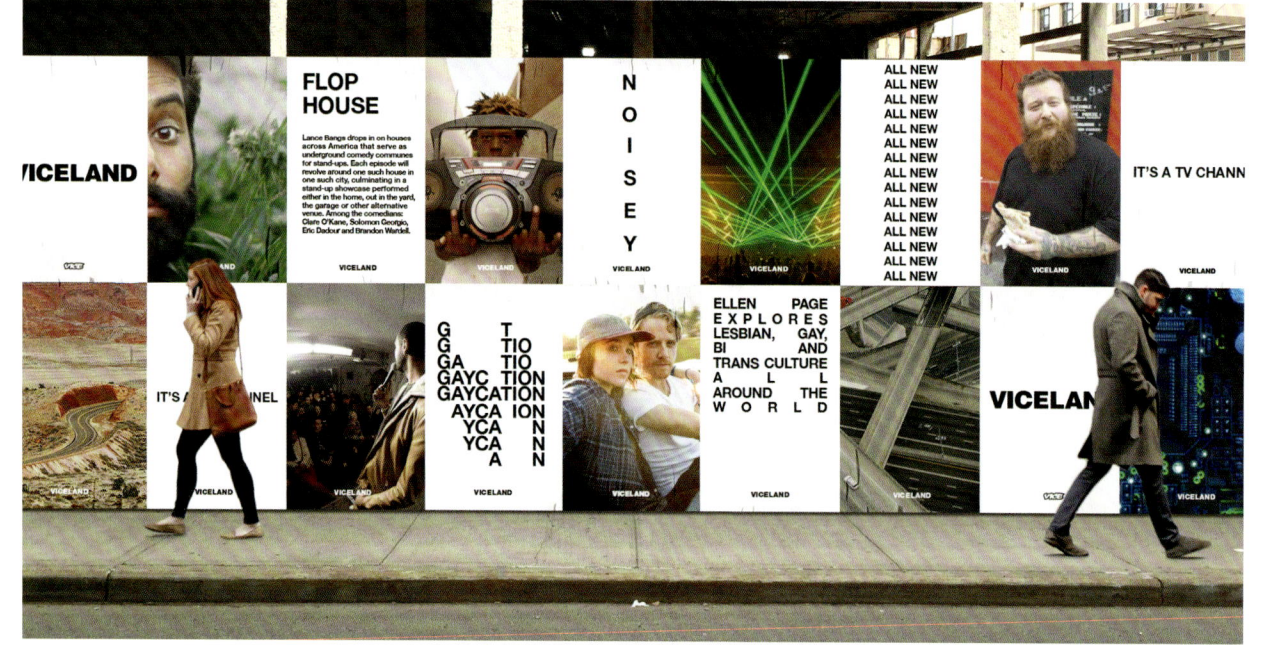

Gretel's work for Viceland (this page and opposite) exemplifies the value of a strong brand proposition and the roles of clear, consistent guidelines to support it. Viceland, with its emphasis on the cultural spectrum, including politics, fashion, sex, music and sport, needed a brand that acts as a containing vehicle, allowing the content to be the main emphasis of the channel.

Viceland defines its brand as 'equal parts exhibition catalog and street flyer; Craigslist and couture; generic and refined. It is simultaneously the elevated 'high' and vernacular 'low'.

The guidelines (top opposite) took the form of a series of printed pamphlets, each focusing on one key aspect of the brand. The use of content is then articulated through the contrast with the strong use of intentional typographic forms.

Sustainability

Graphic design is at the forefront of innovations in sustainability – but has equally been responsible for its fair share of wastage and over-resourcing. This is currently being addressed both in advances in printing processes, and in consumer habit changes.

Advances in printing now enable short print-runs of high quality (gone are the days of digital printing being plagued by streaks of flat colour and lack of definition), which arguably reduces waste. Additionally, it is now possible to print Spot UV and foil digitally, reducing the need for heat-based processes and expensive metal foil blocks.

It is now the norm for traditional printing houses to use recycled stocks, offer carbon-neutral printing and use vegetable-based inks in place of chemical-based ones.

Risograph
A risograph is a low-impact (environmentally), high-speed (it can print up to 130 pages per minute in two colours) digital duplicator, designed by the RISO Kagaku Corporation in 1986. Originally developed for use in schools, clubs and small organisations producing cheap literature in basic colours (it only prints two colours at a time), they are now widely adopted by artists and designers.

The machine is roughly the size of a photocopier, and indeed looks similar to one. The main difference is that the prints produced (for making books, magazines and fanzines etc.) look and feel like silk-screen prints – but can be produced on mass, at low cost and with less environmental impact than traditional lithographic printing. A further important difference between a risograph and a photocopier is that it uses vegetable-based (soy) inks, as opposed to the standard photocopier toners which use plastics, carbon powder and iron oxide, which in some studies have been linked to asthma and other health conditions. As it uses vegetable-based inks and doesn't need to use heat (like a photocopier does) to cure, or seal the pages, it is inherently less environmentally impactful.

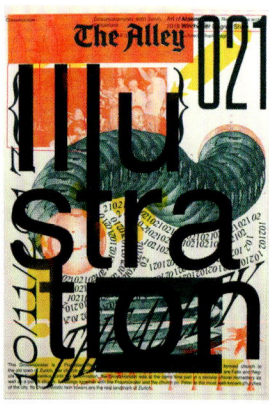

Pictured above and opposite is a self-initiated project by designer **Lukas Keysell** called **OVERPRINT**. The large-format magazine uses a risograph printer to overprint multiple times, allowing for 'happy accidents' to occur. The textural layering and 'collisions' of content create an interesting and novel way of exploring the limits of a printing technique.

Appropriating technology

The contemporary designer sits at a distinct juncture of design innovation, simultaneously interested in technological advances, and the nostalgic methods of the past.

Designers are looking to both the future and the past, but perhaps the most interesting aspect of this particular time of design history is the ability to combine these technological epochs. Arguably, the skill of the designer to seamlessly work across media, irrespective of time, is one of the greatest and most transferable of skills.

Shown below and opposite is a font, A23D commissioned by **Richard Ardagh** of **New North Press**. The 3D-printed letterpress font, designed by **Scott Williams** and **Henrik Kubel** of **A2-Type** connects the newest and the oldest forms of print technology.

Chapter 2 / Context

Adding value and collectability

We inherently collect; it is a facet of human nature and something designers tap into. Having strategies for instilling a sense of collectability in a design can ultimately make a product more desirable and 'valued'.

Interest and collectability can be added to a publication by having multiple covers. This is common in magazine design, where special editions are released with a series of different covers. The eclectic nature of the book shown on these pages makes it all the more personal and desirable. Similar examples can also be seen on pages 176–7 of this book, where a linocut book has a special hand-coloured edition, and on page 99 with a magazine that prints with and without images – with the one without images being the more valued!

You Can Find Inspiration in Everything* This book (opposite) for British clothing designer **Paul Smith**, designed by **Aboud Sodano**, is quite an interesting package. It came in a polystyrene case with a magnifying glass and a pattern for a suit jacket with multiple arms.

The book itself has several tip-ins and multiple covers. The main picture shows the introduction page that has been cut to a different height than the regular pages and is written in multiple languages. The theme of the publication is discovery and excitement, which is certainly portrayed through the various format choices made.

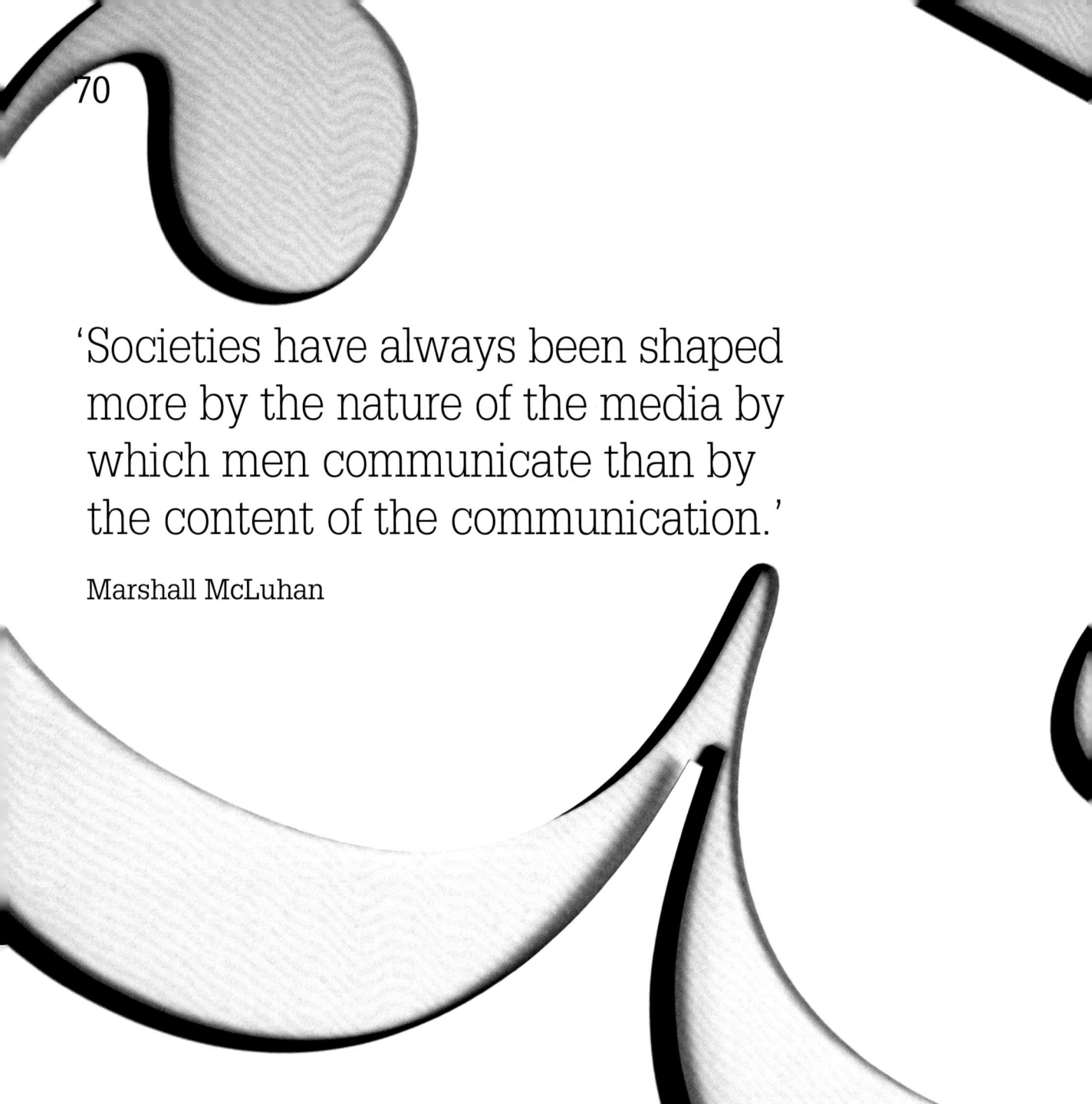

'Societies have always been shaped more by the nature of the media by which men communicate than by the content of the communication.'

Marshall McLuhan

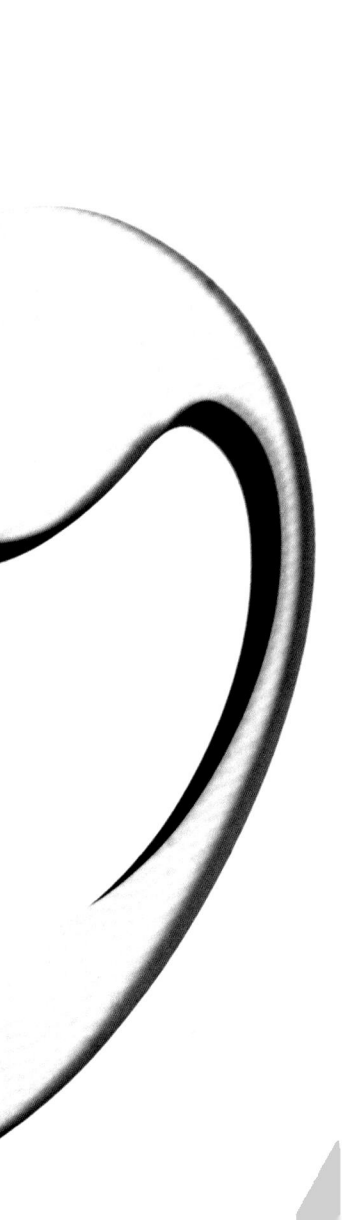

Chapter 3
Printed media

Some of the most important parts of history have been marked by the production of printed matter. From the Magna Carta through to the political propaganda posters of the twentieth century, printed matter is of unrivalled importance and stature.

Alongside these works of national and international importance, our cultural make-up is also constructed by the printed ephemera that surrounds us. Some printed items are intended to be kept as a record, as a cultural marker in time. There is also a plethora of printed items that are transitory and temporary in nature.

This section looks at the many outputs of printed media, from the book through to brochures and posters. The choice of format here is varied and often unconventional – with designers challenging the norms and conventions of any given media.

Standard sizes

Confusingly, design has evolved to run several different systems of standardisation, as described in the tables below and on the following spread.

In essence, book publishing formats are loosely based around standard paper sizes (imperial) that are folded and trimmed. **Folio** refers to pages that have been folded only once, **quarto** editions are formed by folding the paper twice and **octavo** is folded three times. Running concurrent with this, stationery and posters are based generally on either the ISO paper sizes (metric) or the US paper sizes, as shown on the following spread.

Name	Metric (mm)	Imperial (in)
Demy	229 x 152	9 x 6
Royal	235 x 191	9 1/4 x 7 1/2
Crown Royal	280 x 210	11 x 8 1/4
Classic hardback or C format paperback	222 x 143	8 3/4 x 5 5/8
'Trade' paperback or B format	198 x 129	8 x 5 1/4
Imperial folio	390 x 550	15 1/2 x 22
Royal folio	320 x 500	12 1/2 x 20
Imperial quarto	280 x 300	11 x 15
Crown folio	250 x 300	10 x 15
Royal quarto	250 x 320	10 x 12 1/2
Medium quarto	240 x 300	9 1/2 x 12
Demy quarto	220 x 290	8 3/4 x 11 1/4
Foolscap folio	210 x 340	8 1/2 x 13 1/2
Imperial octavo	190 x 280	7 1/2 x 11
Crown quarto	190 x 250	7 1/2 x 10
Foolscap quarto	170 x 210	6 3/4 x 8 1/2
Royal octavo	150 x 250	6 1/4 x 10
Medium octavo	150 x 240	6 x 9 1/2
Demy octavo (demy 8vo)	143 x 222	5 5/8 x 8 3/4
Large crown octavo	129 x 198	5 1/4 x 8
Crown octavo	127 x 190	5 x 7 1/2
Foolscap octavo	108 x 171.5	4 1/4 x 6 3/4
'A' format 'Pulp fiction'	111 x 175	4 1/4 x 6 7/8

Shown here (right) is an annual report, designed by **Thirteen**, for **Bristol Regeneration Partnership.** The design comprises an A5-format book stitched into its own mailable self-sealing greyboard envelope. Being perforated, the top and bottom flaps can be removed upon receipt, so that the object sheds its postal skin and functions purely as a book.

ISO and US paper sizes

The ISO paper size A standard is a system that allows easy enlarging or reducing from one size to the next. Each size is half of the size of the previous one, when folded parallel to the shorter lengths. The ratio of the length to the width is the square root of 2.

In contrast, the ANSI system (American National Standards Institute) has paper sizes based around the Letter (8.5 in x 11 in) format. Unlike the ISO standard sizes which have the single aspect ratio, ANSI standard sizes have two aspect ratios 1:1.2941 and 1:1.5455. This means that enlarging and reducing between sizes leaves irregular gaps and margins. The ANSI system is used in North America, Canada and parts of Mexico. The ISO system is generally adopted in other parts of the world.

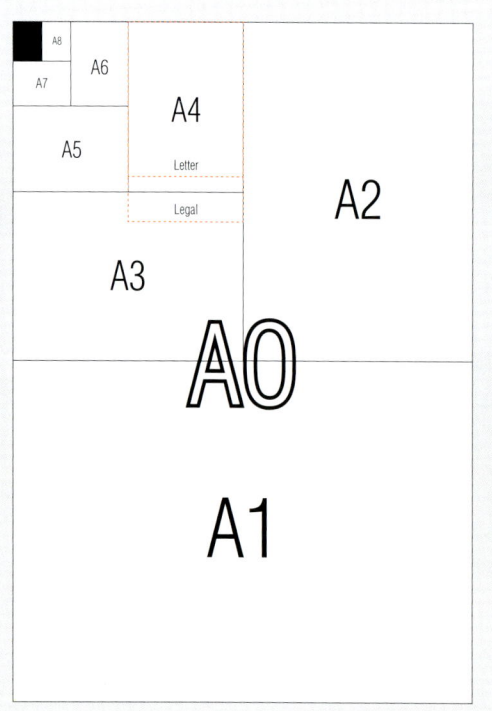

Name	Metric (mm)	Imperial (in)
ISO Paper Sizes		
4A0	2378 x 1682	93.6 x 66.2
2A0	1682 x 1189	66.2 x 46.8
A0	1189 x 841	46.8 x 33.1
A1	841 x 594	33.1 x 23.4
A2	594 x 420	23.4 x 16.5
A3	420 x 297	16.5 x 11.7
A4	297 x 210	11.7 x 8.3
A5	210 x 148.5	8.3 x 5.8
A6	148.5 x 105	5.8 x 4.1
A7	105 x 74	4.1 x. 2.9
A8	74 x 52	2.9 x 2.0
A9	52 x 37	2.0 x 1.5
A10	37 x 26	1.5 x 1.0
US Paper Sizes		
Letter	216 x 279	8.5 x 11
Legal	216 x 356	8.5 x 14
Ledger	279 x 432	11 x 17
Super A3	330 x 483	13 x 19

Karlssonwilker Inc. designed this piece to announce the opening of its design studio. It is a poster (571 mm x 800 mm or 22.5 in x 31.5 in, so slightly smaller than A1) on newsprint, with three parallel folds and a cross fold to reduce it to one-sixteenth in size to enable it to fit into envelopes for mailing.

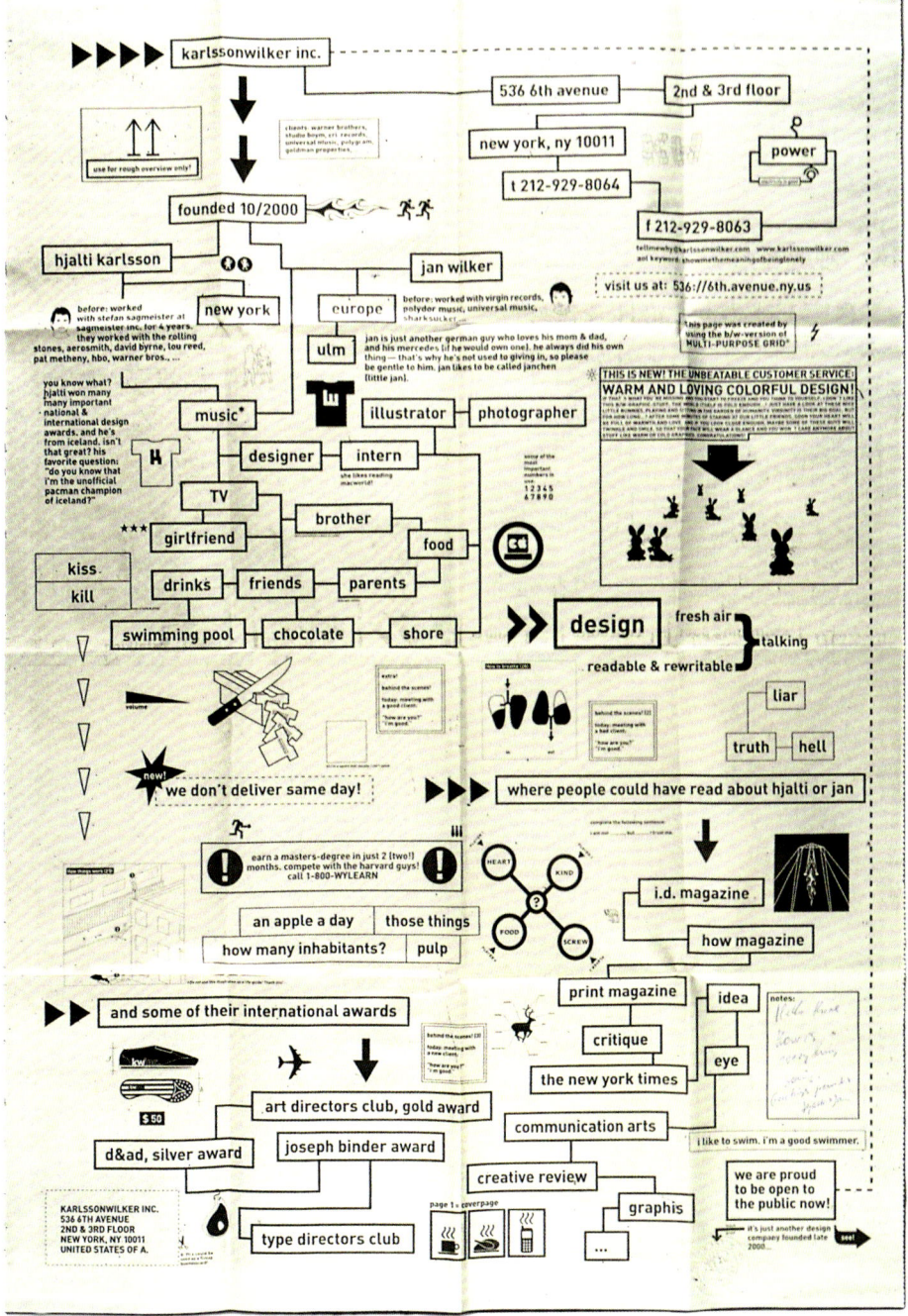

76

An invitation (left) for artist **Luke Morgan** by **Studio Myerscough** that makes a dramatic statement on a utilitarian substrate.

Printed envelopes (opposite) by **Morag Myerscough**, for **Her House**, the studio owner's gallery/shop. An envelope, and certainly the back of an envelope, is a rarely used format on which to place design. By using standard (in this case DL) sized envelopes, the budget for the job can be invested in innovative design and printing rather than in the production of bespoke sized envelopes.

The C series refers to envelope sizes, and these are calculated to hold both folded and unfolded sheets of A sized paper. For example, a C4 envelope holds a sheet of unfolded A4, a C5 envelope holds the same paper folded once and a C6 envelope holds A4 folded twice.

Although we don't naturally think of the humble envelope as affording creativity, the examples on this page go to show that creativity can be applied to the utilitarian pre-bought envelope.

Name	Metric (mm)	Imperial (in)
C0	917 x 1297	36.1 x 51.5
C1	648 x 917	25.5 x 36.1
C2	458 x 648	18.0 x 25.5
C3	324 x 458	12.8 x 18.0
C4	229 x 324	9.0 x 12.8
C5	162 x 229	6.4 x 9.0
C6	114 x 162	4.5 x 6.4
C7	81 x 114	3.2 x 4.5
C8	57 x 81	2.2 x 3.2
C9	40 x 57	1.6 x 2.2
C10	28 x 40	1.1 x 1.6
DL	110 x 220	3.9 x 8.2

rpet dog (Rover) at her house
andrew poulter – a dog can be for christm
at her house
a dog can be for christmas
(Luis) at her house
poulter – a dog can be for christm

Stocks

The feel of printed items has an effect on how we respond to them, and on how we build a sense of identity and brand. Having a good knowledge of how stocks fold and print can help a designer create appropriate and engaging designs.

Standard paper uses

Paper type	Notes	Primary uses
Newsprint	Paper made primarily of mechanically ground wood pulp, shorter lifespan than other papers, cheap to produce, least expensive paper that can withstand normal printing processes.	Newspapers, comics
Antique	Roughest finish offered on offset paper.	To add texture to publications such as annual reports
Uncoated wood-free	Largest printing and writing paper category by capacity that includes almost all office and offset grades used for general commercial printing.	Office paper (printer and photocopy paper, stationery)
Mechanical	Produced using wood pulp, contains acidic lignins. Suitable for short-term uses as it will 'yellow' and colours will fade.	Newspapers, directories
Art board	Uncoated board.	Cover stock
Art	A high-quality paper with a clay filler to give a good printing surface, especially for half-tones where definition and detail are important. Has high brightness and gloss.	Colour printing, magazines
Cast coated	Coated paper with a high-gloss finish obtained while the wet-coated paper is pressed or cast against a polished, hot, metal drum.	High-quality colour printing
Chromo	A waterproof coating on a single side, intended for good embossing and varnishing performance.	Labels, wrappings, and covers
Cartridge	A thick white paper used particularly for pencil and ink drawings.	To add texture to publications such as annual reports
Greyboard	Lined or unlined board made from waste paper.	Packaging material
Flock	Paper coated with flock; very fine woollen refuse or vegetable fibre dust that gives a velvety or cloth-like appearance.	Decorative covers

Designers use a wide range of substrates in brochure design to harness the diverse textures and tactile qualities available, or to benefit from the superior printability of some paper grades, as this brochure called 'London: Cloudy' by **SEA** for the paper manufacturer **MoDo** illustrates. The designers were ultimately trying to engage with print buyers so needed to create something intriguing. The dramatic photography of Richard Green fulfills this narrative role and creates a point of interest to engage with the viewer, while also reflecting the qualities of the textured stocks.

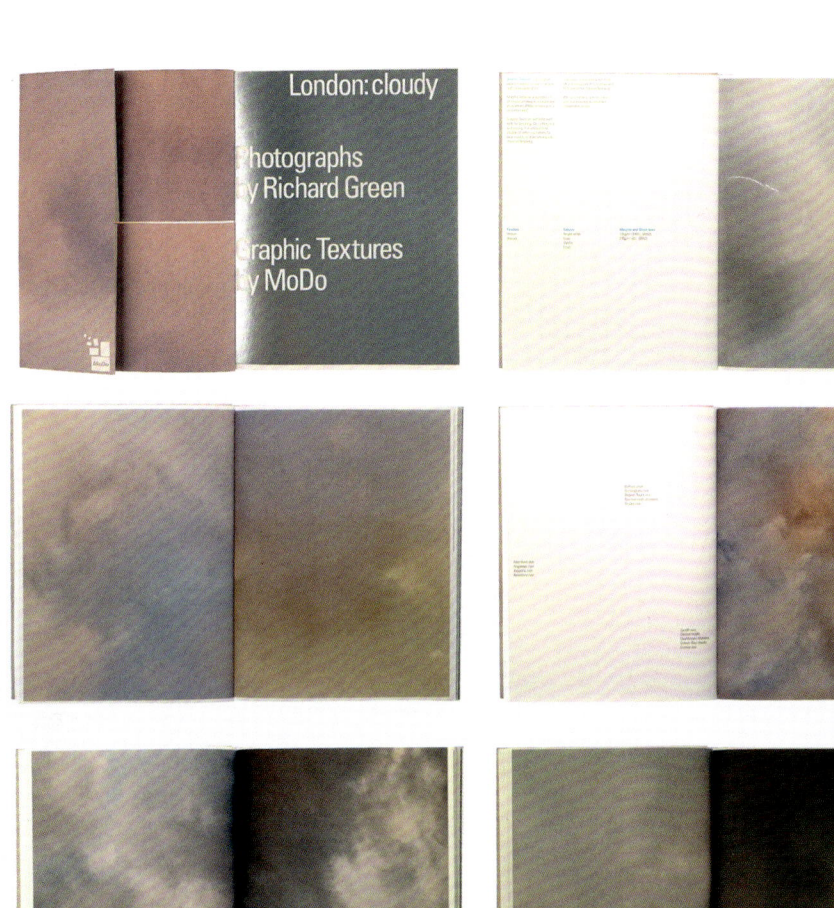

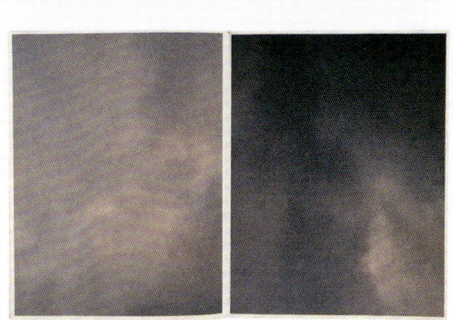

Imposition and multiple stocks

With a simple four-colour job, imposition is not important as every page prints with the same four process colours. If you have the budget or the chance to alter the colour fall, however, such as by using a special colour or spot varnish, more intricate planning may be necessary. You will need to know which pages will need to carry the spot colour by means of an imposition plan.

If you open a book, page 1 obviously backs-up with page 2, page 3 with 4, page 5 with 6 and so on. When specifying colour fall, remember this and it should be straightforward. In the first 16-page section above, pages 1, 4, 5, 8, 9, 12, 13 and 16 print together, with the remaining pages printing on the reverse. This means that these two groups of eight pages can be treated separately, as shown in section 6 opposite, printed in a special colour.

An imposition plan can be used to organise content within the physical format of a book, and to specify paper types and special printing requirements.

The value of planning

An imposition plan provides an economic benefit by reducing the number of sections that you need to print with the special colour. This plan also allows you to maximise the coverage of a special colour; for example, pages 81, 84, 85, 88, 89, 92, 93 and 96 of this book all print with an additional fifth colour, Pantone 805. On an imposition plan, these would all fall on the same side of one 16-page section.

In the example below, a book designed by **Gavin Ambrose** titled **'Objects for – and other things'** by artist Phyllida Barlow for **Black Dog Publishing**, multiple stocks have been used to divide the content. The front section of the book prints on a white stock, while bibliographies and additional information prints on a Kraft stock, black only, spliced in sections throughout the book.

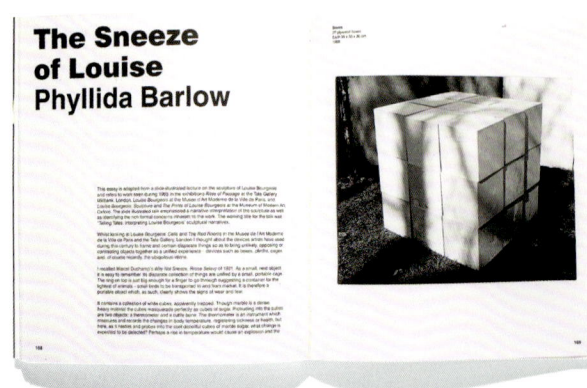

Imposition is a visual representation or guide of how a publication will print. This book prints to the imposition plan shown below. Because it is bound in 16-page sections, there are eight pages to view (eight pages on each side of the sheet). It is specified as a 208-page book with two sections printing on wood-free stock.

The eighth section, on pages 113–128, prints on a wood-free stock, offering a change of texture. The tenth section, on pages 145–160, prints on a wood-free stock, that has been pre-printed with a flat pastel Pantone colour (9100). This is often a more cost-effective way of achieving a 'coloured' stock. Applying a full coverage of a flat colour is often called flood-printing.

1	2	3	4	5	6	7	8	9	10	11	12	13	14	15	16
17	18	19	20	21	22	23	24	25	26	27	28	29	30	31	32
33	34	35	36	37	38	39	40	41	42	43	44	45	46	47	48
49	50	51	52	53	54	55	56	57	58	59	60	61	62	63	64
65	66	67	68	69	70	71	72	73	74	75	76	77	78	79	80
81	82	83	84	85	86	87	88	89	90	91	92	93	94	95	96
97	98	99	100	101	102	103	104	105	106	107	108	109	110	111	112
113	114	115	116	117	118	119	120	121	122	123	124	125	126	127	128
129	130	131	132	133	134	135	136	137	138	139	140	141	142	143	144
145	146	147	148	149	150	151	152	153	154	155	156	157	158	159	160
161	162	163	164	165	166	167	168	169	170	171	172	173	174	175	176
177	178	179	180	181	182	183	184	185	186	187	188	189	190	191	192
193	194	195	196	197	198	199	200	201	202	203	204	205	206	207	208

Notes can be applied to the imposition plan to aid in printing. For example, page 15 of this book carries a full bleed black page that the printer should be made aware of.

Fluorescent 805 prints on pages 81, 84–5, 88–9, 92–3 and 96.

Section 8 prints on wood-free stock.

Section 10 prints on wood-free stock, 'flood printed' with pastel Pantone 9100.

Final 16-page section.

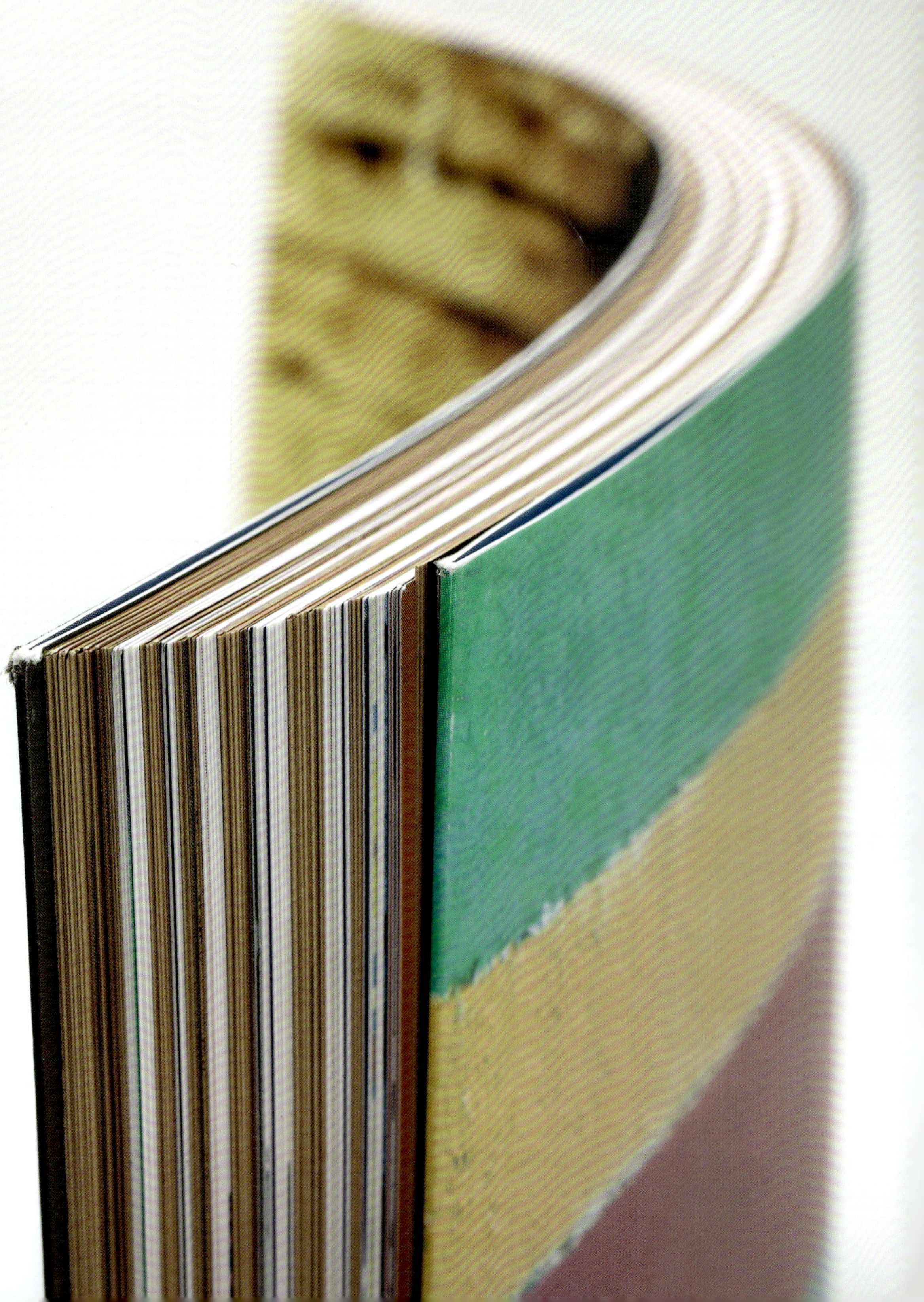

'The Beatles – The True Beginnings', designed by **Rose Design** for **Spine Publishing** (above and opposite), divided two distinct types of information using different stocks. A brown-coloured, uncoated stock carries archival photography and the main text sections. A plain silk stock carries a series of large quotes and non-archival photography by Sandro Sodano. The two stocks enhance the contrast between the high quality of Sodano's studio photography, and the mixed quality of the archival images. The book is formed of fourteen 8-page, four-colour sections on silk stock; and eleven 8-page, two-colour sections on uncoated stock, that are printed and spliced to create the mixed pagination.

Book as sculpture

The book has long since been revered as an object of art and beauty – and not merely as a collection of bound pages.

The shape, form and materials used to construct, cover or add to a standard book can all help to make it feel like more of a product or object. Over the following pages, we look at some striking examples of sculptural books and designs.

Jim Holt and **Trevor Lough** stuck as close to the theme as possible for this brochure (below) for **Pepe Jeans** – by basing the design around a pair of jeans. The cover substrate is denim cloth, with a jeans label on the inside. The tactile quality of the cover makes a strong sculptural statement.

Exquisite corpse
Exquisite corpse, also known as 'exquisite cadaver' is a technique originally developed by the surrealists. It is now often used to describe a book where the pages are cut to intentionally allow juxtaposition.

This brochure (below) by **KesselsKramer** for **Hans Brinker Budget Hotel Amsterdam** has pages cut through the middle to create separate components that can be independently flipped, under a flock cover. The theme of the imagery is that the guests are fine when they arrive but look the worse for wear when they leave, having had such a good time in Amsterdam. The separation allows an interactive juxtaposition of before-and-after images. The sculptural quality is enhanced with the addition of a flock cover, as described on page 198 of this book.

This is a brochure for NatWest Media Centre at the Lord's Cricket Ground in London by **Future Systems. Cartlidge Levene** designed a thick, covered board that forms a folder with a diagonal cut for an opening that wraps around the two sections that comprise the main body. Inside are two loose-leaf sections; one provides a photographic record of the construction project, while the other provides background information about it.

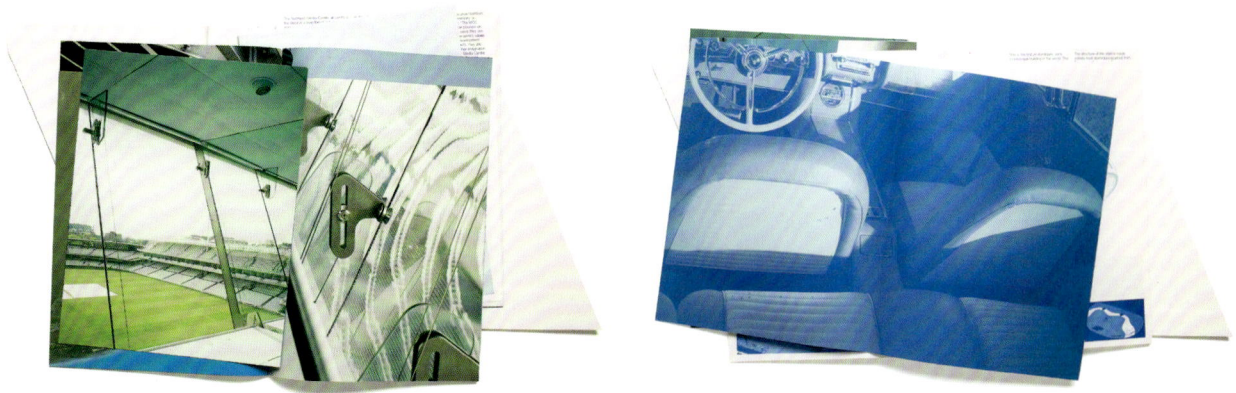

The removal of stock via a die cut (above) opens up a host of visual possibilities in a design. In this example for a **Corbis** image library catalogue by **Segura Inc.**, the cover is die cut with the shapes of several common objects. Laying this over the images within the catalogue shows what an image would look like as a sofa, a vase, a cup and so on, opening up new avenues for image experimentation by the stock photography purchaser.

Each fashion season throws up different themes that need to be worked into the designs that promote the clothing. The theme for this press brochure (left) for **Levi's RED** was glass. **The Kitchen**, therefore, used die-cut pages to reduce the photography of Tim Bret-Day to shards, creating an unusual piece that sits in harmony with the season's theme.

In its design scheme for a book about the industrial design studio Boym & Partners for **Princeton Architectural Press**, **Karlssonwilker Inc.** killed two birds with one stone by putting a die-cut hole in the front cover. In addition to providing a glimpse inside the book, the removed cover stock was used as the book-launch party's invite and a drinks coaster. The design also includes an innovative carry handle hidden between the centre pages.

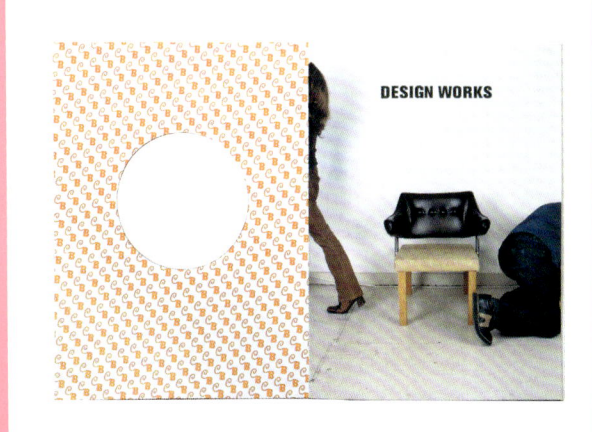

Extensions of the book
The structure and form of a book afford great possibilities in experimentation and expression of narrative or brand. Books often have additional decoration or functional items associated with them, and subverting these elements can be used to create distinctive and memorable designs. This spread shows two examples: the use of a bookmark, above, and the elaborate repurposing of a reader's ribbon, opposite. In both of these designs, the subversion of a book extension item creates a sense of individuality and purpose.

This book (above) for refurbished apartments at 66 St John Street in London was designed by **Studio Myerscough** for **Ivory Gate Limited**. Surreal images are used on a bookmark that has been die cut to the outline of the building's shape. It provides a contrast with the more traditionally informative elements, building plans and alike, that are contained under a series of gatefolds.

Why Not Associates made a useful enhancement to the format of architect Nigel Coates' book '**Ecstacity**' published by **Laurence King** by including several coloured page marker ribbons. The markers highlight the complex dynamics and multiple narratives which characterise today's urban metropolis, which are the focus of this book.

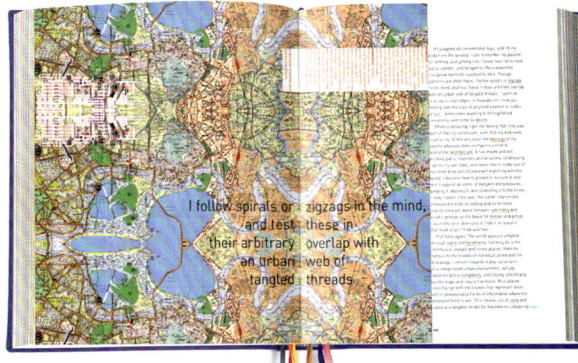

Scale

Scale can have a dramatic effect on a design, making an item instantly more interesting. Making an intentional choice through scale can make a tangible point of difference, marking your design out from the crowd.

Design, by its very nature, is essentially a human activity. We don't just look at design, we interact with it, hold it, carry it with us. For this reason, scale has a very important impact on the way we respond to and interact with printed items. A piece of oversized print has very different connotations compared with a small intimate item, so selecting the appropriate scale can have an influence on how we read and interpret meanings.

For a self-initiated publication, **'Trans>form'**, (opposite) containing images of cranes on the skyline, **Fl@33** chose a loose-leaf oversized magazine format. The format selection marries with the oversized scale of the machinery depicted in the photographs.

A mailer (below) for copywriter **Scott Perry** by **Hat-trick** that has a series of pages specially cut as small as a single line.

Chapter 3 / Printed media

Newspapers

Newspapers were popularised in the seventeenth century as a cheap way of disseminating information en masse. Although the printed newspaper is now in decline, the format remains popular with a new wave of designers and consumers.

Online trends

It would be easy to assume the way we consume 'news' has changed dramatically, going from a bought physical item to a free or subscription-based online delivery. The reality is slightly more complex and is linked to both quality and cost. More people access free news online, and overall printed newspapers have been in decline. However, there are cases of high-quality newspapers (non-tabloid) that are increasing in sales. This is in part to do with modernisation of formats – moving to more modern, easier to carry and read formats, and a change in consumer habits, with an increase in lighter Saturday-based publications as opposed to the traditional full Sunday editions.

Appropriation of format

Changes in digital printing and printing on demand now mean there are many suppliers that offer short-run, low cost 'newspaper' formats. These have appropriated the form and scale of the traditional newspaper and are now a popular choice for self-promotional materials (see following spread). The ability to print as little as a single copy at a reasonable price allows for the content to be changed more regularly and even created for a single reader, client or pitch.

A common production size roughly appropriates the popular 'Berliner' format, which is roughly 315 mm by 470 mm (12.4 in × 18.5 in). The format is narrower and shorter than the oversized broadsheet size, and is therefore easier to handle and read. The Berliner format, as the name suggests, was created in Berlin in contrast to the larger French and North German sizes. This format has been adopted by many traditionally broadsheet newspapers in a move to modernise and popularise their format.

The early days of digital printing were marred by poor quality and unsaturated images, but increases in printing resolution (up to 600 dpi) now sees publications being printed in high quality, at low cost and on demand.

This design by **Frost*** for **'Ampersand'** (opposite), a **D&AD** newsletter, borrows heavily from newspapers in terms of its format, scale, design and typography, which includes Jim-dashes (short rules dividing information), kickers (lines of copy appearing above or below an article), necklines (white spaces under running heads), standfirsts (introductory paragraphs), and mastheads (titles and visual keystones of a publication).

The use of this format lends the presented information a currency and authority that compels people to read it.

Denotation and connotation

All formats communicate on two main levels: denotation and connotation, and the appropriation of a format can successfully exploit this. For example, on a denotative level, a newspaper is simply a large-format piece of print, usually on a cheap light stock. However, on a connotative level it implies it is 'newsworthy', it is journalistic, it will have an opinion and is true.

In the example shown on this page, designer and illustrator **Matt Chase** used the newspaper format for the creation of a self-promotional mailer entitled **'Some Things I Have Made'**. A simple hierarchy of text and image is instilled through the use of an overprinted narrative running through the publication.

The clever appropriation of this format, on a connotative level, invites the recipient, through the familiarity of the format, to 'read' it.

Some Things I Have Made

Magazines

The magazine has become an artistic expression of ideas and form. Narrative is often dominated by images and the sequence that these are presented in. The magazine format offers a lot of scope for creative experimentation.

Pioneering magazine **Tank** takes many forms – be it playing with scale and form, or pushing the boundaries of content. Shown opposite is an issue called 365 days later, that was printed at an unusually small size. Shown left is a special edition available without images, and the corresponding mainstream issue that came complete with images.

This challenging of format and media has seen the rise of the magazine as a form to be celebrated in its own right, as a symbol of personal expression and experimentation.

Toko's design work for **The Code Magazine** dates back nearly a decade, when they first designed the masthead and initial issue. Subsequent issues have used a variety of different layouts, bespoke typefaces and special sections of editorial content. The Code Magazine reports on style and fashion through the use of 'real' people, giving the publication a point of difference in the style magazine department. The avant-garde and sometimes reportage approach taken has led to The Code Magazine becoming a platform for emerging designers and brands.

The magazine uses a variety of grids, typefaces and page layouts to create a sense of pace and dynamism.

FROM BERLIN WITH LUV

Posters

Posters surround us – on billboards, buses and taxis, they are endemic to the urban environment.

When designing for posters, arguably the most important consideration is the sense of scale that is required for text and image to be readable. It is also important to keep the message, or intent, of the poster simple enough to be understood quickly and from a distance. The poster format has also been reconfigured to wrap around books and publications, as shown on page 108 of this book.

This poster for **Creative Review** magazine was designed by **Angus Hyland** at **Pentagram** to promote a student subscription offer. The message invited people to reconstruct the poster. Made up of a double sheet, with a fold along the top edge, each letter is perforated through the middle to provide an element of interaction: as they are removed, details of the subscription are revealed.

Neo Neo used the subtlety of printing techniques in the poster for an international film festival, **Black Movie** (opposite), in Geneva. Glossy black ink overprints matt black ink to create a richly textured effect and memorable identity. As with any design, the context within which the design will be placed is as important as the design itself.

Shown here (below) are posters from **Boy Bastiaens** digital sketchbook, as part of an exhibition called **Shapes & Things** held in the attics of the Maastricht Central Station. The posters are visual outputs of happy accidents and consider the role of coincidence and inspiration in the design process.

Chapter 3 / Printed media

Poster wraps
A poster wrap is used to form a loose, informal cover that can be removed and opened out to reveal a poster format. It combines the practicalities of a dust jacket with the scale and effect of the poster.

Rather than create a publication with a spine for the prospectus for **Ravensbourne University London**, **MadeThought** created a folded poster wrap that opens to reveal a student hard at work. This is in stark contrast to the majority of prospectuses that normally have a similar format to this book. The format used also allows the information to be arranged according to the folded panels, bringing a hierarchical order to the piece.

The poster wrap, by its nature, reveals and conceals elements of image and text as it is unfolded. This can be approached in two ways; firstly, by carefully planning where text and image will be in relation to folds. Alternatively, the folding process can be used to introduce an element of chance in the cropping and concealing of images.

The poster is deeply rooted in democratic practice – being the vehicle of choice for agitation and protest for centuries. This small poster festival by **Studio245** features the work of 130 students along a 200-metre stretch of hoarding in Brighton, UK, as part of a redevelopment of the area with **U+I**. Individual posters are combined to make rudimentary letterforms as shown opposite (letter A), which when produced en masse creates a series of statements.

To illustrate how an innovative piece of flexible furniture works, designer **John Rushworth** of **Pentagram** perforated the back page of this exhibition catalogue (above) so that readers can separate and rearrange photos of the pieces, then bind them with an elastic band to create a flip-book that animates the furniture. This low-tech design for the **Crafts Council's** Flexible Furniture exhibition encapsulates animation and a sense of engagement in a simple, well crafted form.

Animation

We often think of animation as being online, in films or cartoons, but a sense of movement can also be instilled into printed matter through paper engineering and materials.

While the dream of moving images on printed paper remains just that, the use of paper and augmented reality has started to become a reality. Printed images can now be viewed as moving images with the use of mobile phone applications and the technology that allows this has become increasingly more affordable and available.

Animation and a sense of movement can be realised through the use of low-tech materials, as per the example opposite in the form of a flip-book complete with elastic band. Alternatively, innovative printing techniques can be employed, as in the example below, where lenticular printing has added movement and depth to the design.

Design studio **North** put a lenticular image, on the front and rear covers of the Design Guidelines Brand Manual for **Telewest** (below). The cover image is the organisation's logo, which moves and changes as the reader changes his or her viewing angle. The idea is very simple but also well-executed, transforming a corporate brochure into an object of desire.

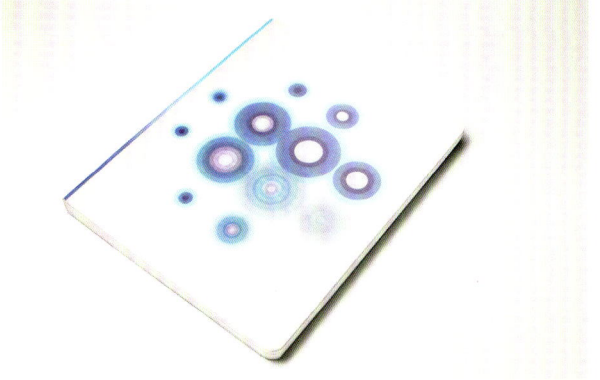
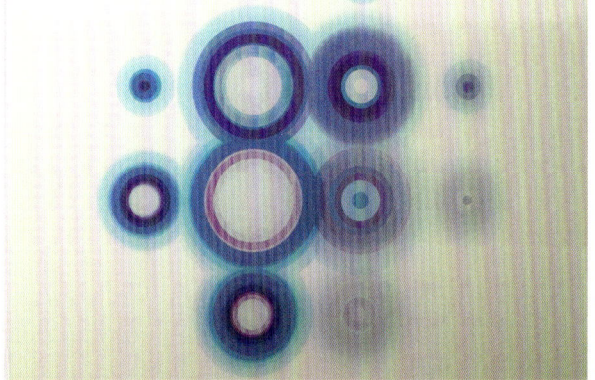
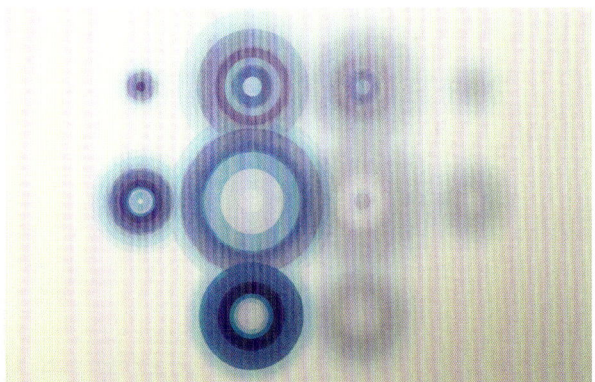
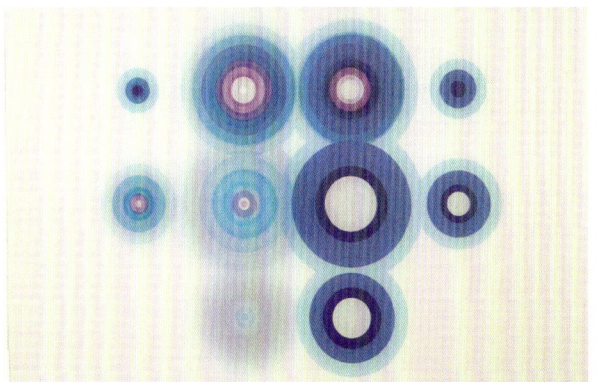

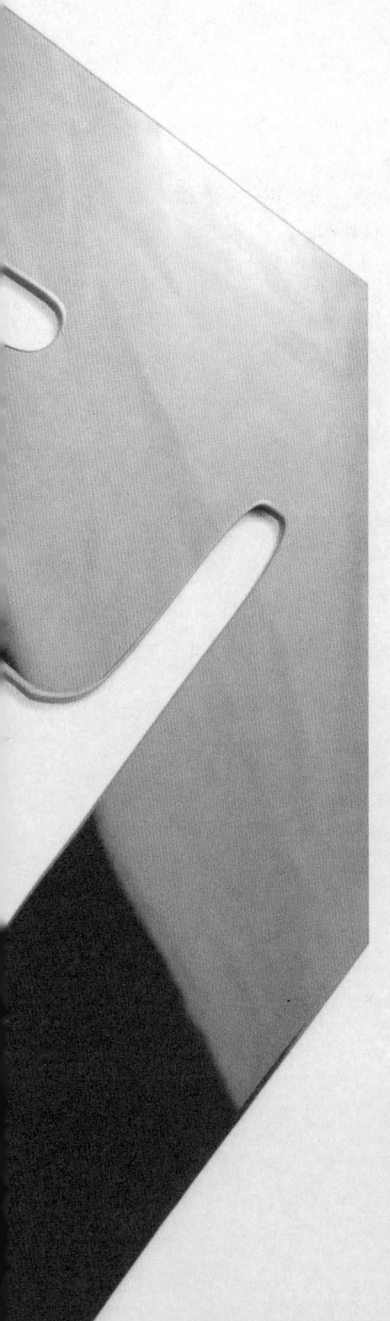

Chapter 4
Folding

We shouldn't underestimate the importance of the simple fold. It is a time-honoured technique that has been widely used in Japanese origami for religious and ceremonial purposes since the sixth century.

Folding techniques can be used to add a sense of interest and uniqueness to a design, but they are also useful 'tools' for dissecting information and controlling pace. Designers use folding methods to compartmentalise information, as well as to order the way in which content is revealed.

We often think of design as being a flat activity, with the results appearing on screen or on paper. By having an understanding of how paper can be manipulated, a sense of craft and engineering can be instilled into a design.

'Design is a funny word. Some people think design means how it looks. But of course, if you dig deeper, it's really how it works.'

Steve Jobs

Making a maquette, or printer's dummy of a design (above) will allow you to see any printing issues in advance, for example, 'creep', where the stock bulks up meaning more bleed is needed on a design. It also allows you to make accurate measurements for the overhang of covers, as in the example opposite. A flat, clean space and a folding bone are essential for accurate folding.

This invite by **NB Studio** to a **BBC Radio & Music Summer Reception** perfectly illustrates the accordion fold (also known as a fan fold). Made from a single sheet of paper, folds are made along its length and then across at a right angle, to make a fan. A printed white substrate was then glued on to the outside.

Maquettes and printer's dummies

Folding may seem simple, and essentially it is, but trying to explain to a client or printer what needs to be done, can become complicated.

The simplest way to avoid any confusion and to ensure that you, your client and printer are all referring to the same type of fold in a design, is to make a maquette, which is a working sample of your design. At a later stage, the printer will often make what is called a 'printer's dummy' – a version of the design, in the right stock and paper weight.

Folding examples

The examples in this book often use folding as a design feature to structure the way content is revealed, and to add pace and interest to designs. Although many of these look complex, they are usually based on simple techniques. Shown opposite are four basic approaches to paper engineering that create a sense of pace and 'reveal'.

In this self-promotional portfolio (below), **Frost Design** adds to the physical texture of a piece and provides a novel way of dividing space or organising elements.

Roll fold – a continuous folding-in, making sure the pages in the middle section are slightly smaller than those on the outer.

Gatefold – double or single gatefolds create a sense of reveal and pace.

Concertina fold – alternating valley and mountain folds create a simple concertina.

Self-covers – folding can be used to create a book and cover all from a single sheet of paper.

Chapter 4 / Folding

Different types of fold

There are many unusual and interesting folding techniques available to add interest to a design.

There are essentially two basic folds used to construct even the most complex of printed items; the 'valley fold' and the 'mountain fold'. A valley fold is created when you fold the paper towards yourself: to make a mountain fold, you fold it behind or away from yourself.

A valley fold creates a 'V' or valley shape. A mountain fold creates an apex shape. From these two basic folds, nearly all printed matter can be constructed. When folding manually, it is always good practice to use a 'bone', as pictured opposite.

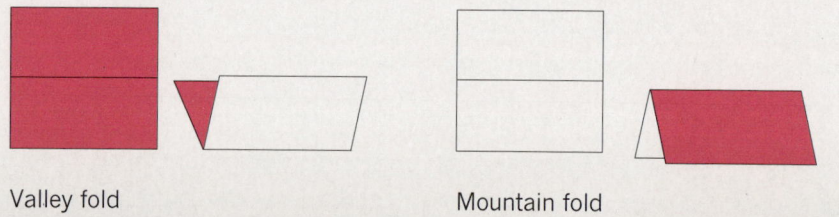

Valley fold   Mountain fold

Valley fold

Folding with a 'bone'

Mountain fold

Chapter 4 / Folding

A selection of common folds

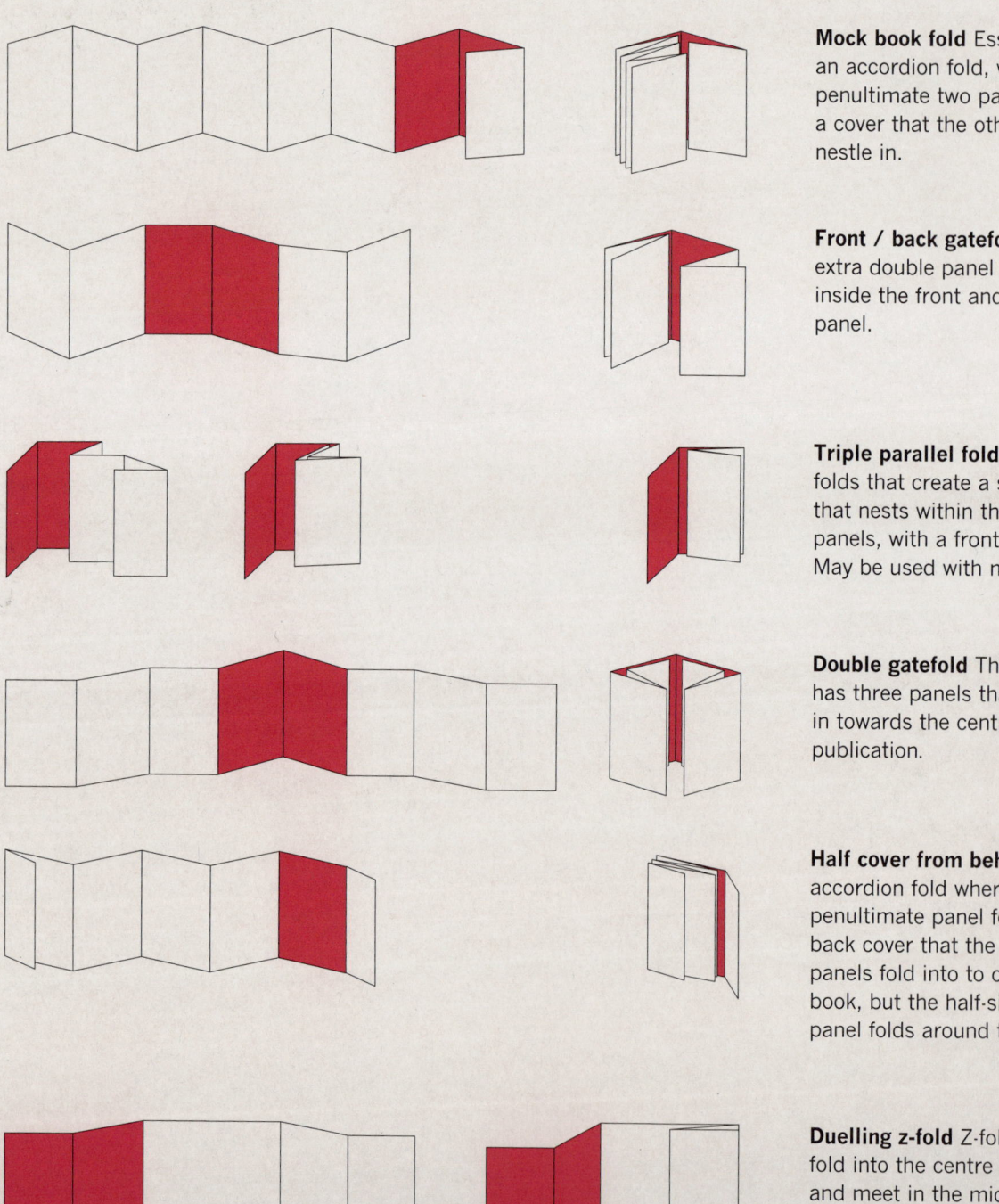

Mock book fold Essentially an accordion fold, where the penultimate two panels form a cover that the other panels nestle in.

Front / back gatefold An extra double panel that folds inside the front and/or back panel.

Triple parallel fold Parallel folds that create a section that nests within the cover panels, with a front opening. May be used with maps.

Double gatefold The gatefold has three panels that fold in towards the centre of the publication.

Half cover from behind An accordion fold where the penultimate panel forms a back cover that the other panels fold into to create a book, but the half-size end panel folds around the book.

Duelling z-fold Z-fold wings fold into the centre panel and meet in the middle.

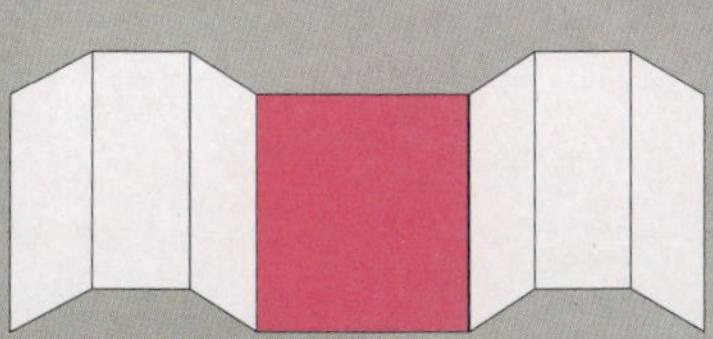

Back / front folder Wings either side of the central panel have a double parallel fold so that they can fold around and cover both sides of the central panel.

Front / back accordion fold With three parallel folds, the two-panel outer wings fold into and out of the centre. The double panel centre serves as the cover.

The basic concertina

A combination of alternating valley and mountain folds creates the basic concertina design.

Each fold runs opposite to the previous one to obtain a pleated result. The outer page needs to be larger than the inner pages to hide the rough folding edges of the final piece.

The amount of extra coverage the outer cover will need to conceal the inners when folded can only be worked out by making a printer's dummy in the correct stock and weight. There are also intentional variations on this, where the front is cut short as opposed to overlapping the inners, creating a juxtaposition of the cover and the panel below.

The cover is usually formed from the same stock as the inners, a so-called 'self-cover', as in the example on this page. A variation is to apply a secondary cover, as in the example on the opposite page.

SEA Design chose to use a concertina fold in its design for a literature system for the UK's **Tate** galleries (right). The fold physically divides up the area into equal manageable 'panels' on which the design can be organised.

Outer page is fractionally larger to hide the pages below

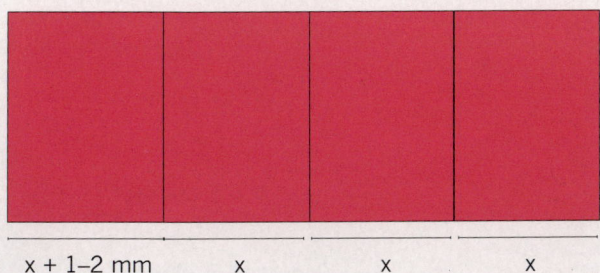

x + 1–2 mm   x   x   x

124

Struktur used a concertina fold to produce a self-promotional calendar entitled '**Minutes**' (this page and opposite). It is almost 3m long when unfolded. The folding method used here provides an obvious benefit as it enables the product to be condensed into a more manageable form, and also provides physical pages upon which to position the design. The length of the calendar meant that it had to be printed in three sections that were fixed together; heavy embossed greyboard ends were then glued on to provide a protective carrier in the form of a self-cover.

Variations on 'self-covers'

A variation of the concertina fold involves a type of self-cover, and is often referred to as a 'harmonica fold'. Variations on this fold can be seen in lots of designs, including the design opposite – where a separate die-cut cover is bonded to the folded inner pages creating a document that the user is encouraged to explore, as opposed to simply read.

Harmonica self-cover fold An accordion fold (below) where the first two panels form a cover that the other panels fold into. The first two panels need to be larger than the others to allow for creep.

For **The Suitcase** project at the Eindhoven Design Academy in the Netherlands (below), **KesselsKramer** created a brochure with a concertina fold to emulate a suitcase – the contents spill out when it is opened. The end page is die-cut so that it can be wrapped around the folded brochure to close it. The brochure documents a project in which students used the possessions from a suitcase to construct a personality for a fictional character.

Combining techniques

Often, a design will use a combination of different folding techniques to create the desired structure. A poster format folded into a concertina brochure (as above) or a book with a concertina section (as opposite), for example. Ultimately, if you can fold it by hand, it can generally be recreated on a commercial scale, and some of these techniques can add a point of difference in a crowded and saturated market.

Bruce Mau Design created this poster (above) for an exhibition on pop artist **Richard Hamilton** at the Gagosian Gallery in London. It is a 32-panel fold-down poster, which, when open, reveals a near life-size image by Rita Donagh of the artist carrying one of his works, 'Epiphany'.

This concertina booklet promoting photographer **Arnhel de Serra** by **Born** design studio makes effective use of contrasting folds. One side features his colour work and the reverse his black and white. The cover features an identity that reflects the photographer's Spanish heritage.

French fold
A sheet of paper that has two right-angle folds to form a 4-page, uncut section. The section is sewn through the fold, while the top edges remain folded and untrimmed. It's common for the inner reveals to be printed with a flood colour or with information, as shown above and opposite.

This spirit guide (a book outlining the aspirations and values of a brand) designed by **North** for stock photography library **The Image Bank** (above), introduces a new identity, typographic style and outlines for image use. As a means to organise information, the guide has a clear yet engaging narrative. The outer face of the folded sheets carries the main messages of the guide, while the inner reveals use increasingly more experimental interpretations of the typographic style. This design also uses a thin stock to enable showthrough, a useful device for making it clear that the pages contain information in the folds.

A French fold is also sometimes produced with a perforated edge, allowing the pages to be separated, as shown opposite.

For this design for **Mind** magazine (opposite), **Tank** used paper accordion-folded into 32-page sections and sewn into a book block. The spine of the book can be seen on page 157 of this book. The outer edge of the pages has a perforated fold, encouraging users to tear open the pages to reveal the hidden prints. Over time this results in the book having a rough, deckle edge print, where the pages have been torn open.

Gatefolds, throw-outs and fold-outs
These terms have become interchangeable, and refer to extra panels that fold into the central spine of a publication. Parallel folds are used so that the panels meet in the middle of the page. The extended pages are folded and cut shorter than the standard publication pages so that they can nest correctly. Gatefolds are commonly used in magazines and in special edition vinyl record covers.

In this example of a gatefold for **Another Magazine** (below and right), a four-panel gatefold features Chris Robinson from the rock group The Black Crowes (above) and actress Kate Hudson (below right), with art direction by Stella McCartney.

Chris Robinson, lead singer of The Black Crowes, has just
completed a world tour promoting his latest album, Lions.

135

This publication for **The Macedonian Museum of Contemporary Art** by the **Design Shop** entitled 'The Gesture. A visual library in progress' makes clever use of a double gatefold cover. This subtle exhibition catalogue takes readers on a journey of discovery. Hidden within the flaps of the book cover, lies a fold-out image which sits in stark contrast to the book's delicate monochrome tonality, unexpectedly displaying a rush of colour but also a strange sense of calm due to the image portrayed.

Chapter 4 / Folding

Throw-ups

A throw-up is a variation on a throw-out, where a folded page, larger than the document that contains it, is folded in allowing it to be opened out. They are often used to showcase a particular image.

Jeans manufacturer **Levi's** entitled its Denim Delinquent book "no" (right and below) after writer Albert Camus's comment that 'a rebel is a man who says no'. To emphasise the rebellion angle, **The Kitchen** staged its own formatting rebellion in the design. Spliced between the pages of the book are nine four-colour throw-ups with a French fold. These feature images of rockers, tomboys and other 'rebels'. The book cover is cloth-bound with embossed lettering.

Iris Associates designed a series of five posters (right and below), or throw-ups, that were folded into six panels for a brochure for the florist **Plantology**. The throw-ups (with one horizontal and two vertical folds) fold out to show striking flower photography. The folded posters are glued between heavyweight foil-blocked boards.

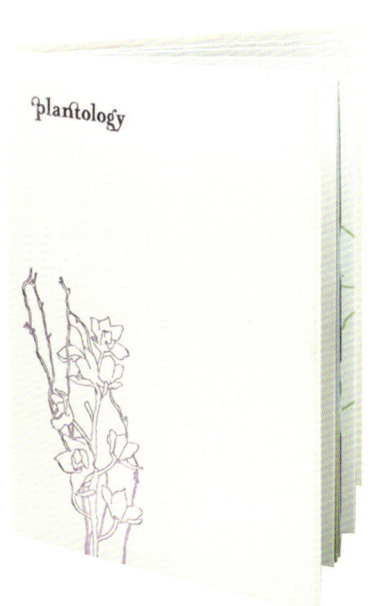

Bellybands

A bellyband is a paper or plastic substrate that is folded around the 'belly' of a publication. The substrate may be a full loop or a strip. Commonly used on magazines, they serve to produce an eye-catching piece of information.

For this catalogue (below) for a Bill Brandt exhibition at the **Focus Gallery** in London, **MadeThought** specified that the central pages should be cut with a shorter width than the multi-panel wrap-cover enclosing it. The front cover folds out so that readers can see information about works in the exhibition as they browse the content pages. The exhibition catalogue was produced with three different bellybands featuring key images from the show.

Endorse fold

An endorse fold is an informal 'additional' fold, applied after a product is finished. It is not creased or scored and is commonly used to make a printed item smaller than its finished sized, for example when folding a broadsheet newspaper in half to make it more manageable to carry.

In this example (left and above), by **Sagmeister Inc.** for **Anni Kuan**, a New York fashion designer, a loose broadsheet brochure hangs on a wire coat hanger on its endorse fold and each page has been subjected to some very bespoke print finishing – by being burnt with an iron! It took five minutes to burn each of the brochure's 16 pages.

Folding as identity

The distinctive nature of folding means it can be used to dramatic effect, forming sharp graphic shapes and patterns. Designers can exploit this distinctive characteristic in designs and especially in the creation of identities.

Simple paper engineering can be used to create strong visual statements. Creating a point of difference is arguably one of the main aims of design, and utilising the tactile nature of paper and paper engineering can produce successful and memorable designs.

This stationery package (below) was designed by **Hat-trick**, and was tailored to the client, **Zuckerman**, using the initial 'Z' of Zuckerman. The format of each item is die-cut on a bias to give a sloping top edge so that when folded – with a z-fold, naturally – the red strip running along the top becomes a 'Z'.

This identity for **West Architecture** by design agency **Morse Studio** (this page) makes explicit use of folding as an integral part of the design. The stationery makes an architectural statement while the brochure features an innovative reverse-folded cover.

Folding for self-containment

Folding can be an effective way of creating self-contained printed items that can be mailed or dispatched without the need for additional packaging.

This can either be in the form of a self-cover, where a single sheet is folded into itself and sealed, or in the form of an applied, separate cover, that is folded around the inners, offering protection and ease of packaging.

The versatility of the mailer format can be seen in this example (opposite and below) by **Frost Design** for the **Photonica** photo library. Catering for the physical size and weight constraints that arise from the fact it is designed for mailing, it sacrifices nothing in terms of creativity or communication. A small selection of the images from the photo library are displayed in the piece, courtesy of a concertina fold pull-out. This folded section is bonded into a card wrap-folder to make it a more convenient size for sending through the post. The four-colour design is perforated, like a sheet of stamps, allowing the images to be separated and used like swatches – and providing an indication of the usage and variety of the full library of images.

'Craft is part of the creative process.'

Gavin Bryars

Chapter 5
Binding

Binding is the process of collecting loose pages into a coherent and contained form, but it is also more important than that – it forms part of the design narrative. The nature, look and feel of a binding mechanism can help in the dissemination of information and can establish the 'tone' of a design, be it formal or informal, high-tech or low-tech.

Although often automated for large printing runs, there are still many forms of binding that can only be done by hand. The very physical nature of this links binding to a sense of craft; the tactile and the human, and arguably this is why we respond to carefully created books with such human interaction.

Binding can also refer to a fabric strip used to seal the edge of a publication, and is also sometimes used to describe the covering of a book.

It is important to remember that a design that involves construction and paper engineering techniques will require more time. This is to enable the designer to liaise with printers and fabricators, and to enable testing and the development of prototypes and maquettes.

This section, pages 145–160, is flood printed with Pantone 9100 as a base colour. This technique is often used as a means of creating the effect of a change of stock but in a more cost-effective manner.

Types of binding

Bookbinding can essentially be categorised as either 'commercial' (large-scale) or 'hand' (small-scale), depending on the complexity and volume produced. Many of the terms used in binding are historic and, as with all forms of design, there is a cycle of fashionability. There is also an infinite number of variations, or more informal binding methods, as shown bottom left and right.

Shown below are some of the many ways binding choice can add interest to a design. The spine of a book is a facet greatly exploited by designers to add a point of difference.

Connotations of binding styles
Bookbinding is primarily the collation of pages, or sections of pages, into an order usually with the addition of a protective covering. Sometimes, however, publications are bound with a self-cover, which is simply a form of binding that uses the same stock for the cover as the inners of the book.

'How' a book is bound also has connotations of how we respond to a design. Is it formal, informal, playful or purposefully hard to use? Is it austere or inviting, rooted in craft or technology, for example? All these considerations are to be taken into account by a designer as they all collectively add to the narrative and sense of order in a design.

For this book, **'City Racing, The Life and Times of an Artist-Run Gallery'**, published by **Black Dog Publishing**, **Society** chose a greyboard cover to add grittiness to the publication and reflect its content. The cover and the endpapers were silk-screened and a green buckram binding applied – buckram is a coarse linen or cotton fabric sized with glue or gum, and used for covering a hardcover binding. The choice of stocks make a unique and powerful statement, as do the choice of typeface and colour.

Common binding techniques

The most common binding methods are edition, perfect and saddle stitch.

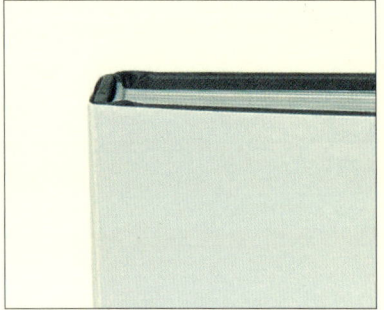

Edition binding Case or edition binding has signatures, or sections, of a book sewn together and bound with a cloth strip down the spine. This is then attached to endpapers, in turn connecting the text block to hard outer covers. This outer cover is then often 'wrapped' in a dust jacket for added protection as in the example below for **Rankin** by **Form**.

Perfect binding A binding method commonly used for paperback books, where the signatures are held together with a flexible adhesive that also attaches a paper cover to the spine. The fore-edge is trimmed flat. Perfect binding is economical and often used for magazine production.

Saddle stitch A binding method used for booklets, programmes and small catalogues. Signatures are nested and wire stitches are applied through the spine along the centrefold. When opened, saddle-stitched books lay flat. Variations on saddle stitch include staples used with an open ring, allowing the contents to be stored in a folder.

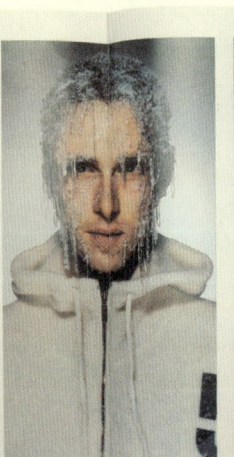

Layflat binding
A variation of perfect binding is a technique called layflat binding, which allows a book to be opened completely flat. As the pages are glued to just the thin edge of the paper, the stock has to be heavy to prevent the pages from simply falling out. This catalogue was produced to accompany **Mikael Eliasson's** solo exhibition, **Resemblance** by **Morse Studio**. The family portraits are printed on a rigid, uncoated card stock and arranged objectively across spreads with a delicate passe partout border. The catalogue is perfect-bound with buckram book-tape covering the spine, enabling the spreads to lie flat when open.

Z-binds

Z-binds use a dual-binding technique, where two books are essentially bound on to a single cover. In the case of a perforated z-bind, these are pre-cut, indicating that the two parts are intended to be separated. Z-binds usually consist of two perfect-bound or saddle-stitched spines and a joining cover, although there are variations on this. Z-binds are very effective at making a clear distinction between types of content, and instill a feeling of exploration and reveal to a design.

As there are two spines, paper-weight and handleability can become an issue and it is advisable to get a 'printer's dummy' or maquette made in advance so you can gauge how the stocks will act and feel. The cover, for example, needs to be sturdy enough to support the two spines while being flexible enough to make the design usable.

This brochure (right) for **Millennium Loft's 9 Kean Street** designed by **Cartlidge Levene** is a two-section publication connected by a perforated z-bind.

The front section uses strong colour photography of Covent Garden by Gueorgui Pinkhassov, who was commissioned by the client to spend a week in Covent Garden to photograph the area. The back section has a more limited colour palette and contains information specific to the twenty-two lofts that comprise the development.

Thinking Big, Concepts for Twenty-first Century British Sculpture (opposite), for Sculpture at Goodwood comprises two parts: the front section contains detailed biographies of the sculptors that created the eighty-five works, while the back section contains atmospheric and abstract imagery by Richard Learoyd. The design, by **Made Thought,** has two sections that share a z-fold cover.

Formal binding

Formal bindings can be categorised as permanent, fixed order bindings that are utilitarian in function and aesthetics.

Wiro/comb binding

The simple wiro bind is arguably the most utilitarian of all binding methods. It is cheap, rigid, and with the addition of heavy outer stocks, or even other substrates as in the example below that uses two metal sheets, has longevity offering a high degree of protection. A spine of metal (wiro) or plastic (comb) rings allows a document to open flat. Often used for reports, office publications and manuals, the plastic version feels cheaper, while specialist metal finishes will add more value to a design.

For this cookbook (below) for **OXO**, **Tank** used a magnetised metal substrate, simply wiro bound so the pages open flat, enabling the cookbook to be stuck to the fridge.

The pages are laminated in order for static electricity to hold them together so that they don't flip over while suspended.

Canadian and half-Canadian binding
In a full Canadian bind, the spirals that contain the document are completely hidden. In a half-Canadian bind (as above) they are left partially exposed. This is essentially a spiral-bound document, but with the advantage of having a book-like spine. As with spiral-bound documents, they have the advantage of laying completely flat when in use.

'Lost Found Time' (above) is a collection of poetry by senior citizens, and was designed by **Eg.G** for **Stockport Arts** and **Health, UK**, It uses a half-Canadian binding to neatly contain the contents.

154

Informal binding

Informal bindings can be described as having a looseness in their construction, for example loose-leaf, where there is little if any structure. In addition, informal bindings use craft-based as opposed to mechanical structures, and often appropriate traditional techniques.

Open binding

Printed matter that has been open bound looks very much like a book without its final cover-board applied. The glue and fabric used to secure pages are left exposed, creating a strong graphic statement as in the example opposite.

This publication (below), by **KesselsKramer** was created for an exhibition held at the former naval dockyard Oude Rijkserf Willemsoord in the Netherlands for **Kaap Helder**. It uses a half-exposed and half-covered open spine. The undersized greyboard cover is glued to the exposed spine, leaving the section sewing exposed, and in turn making a strong visual statement.

Designed by **NB Studio** for **Hub**, a centre for craft design and making in the UK, the book (opposite) is essentially a series of 148 heavyweight postcards bound into a book format. No cover is applied to the spine, which gives the publication a sculptural appearance.

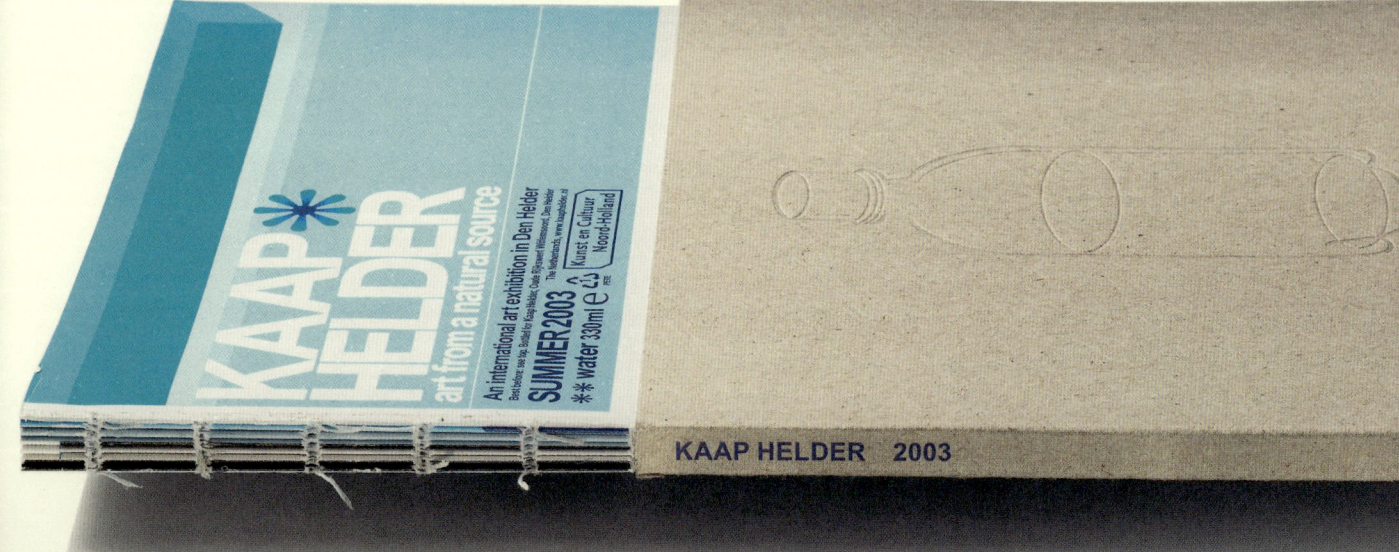

Design agency **Born** used an open bind in the catalogue for the **'Venice Take Away – Ideas to Change British Architecture'** exhibition for the **Architectural Association** (opposite). The utilitarian nature of the open bind reveals the colour coded sections and also allows the book to be opened flat.

In its design for **Mind** magazine (right), **Tank** used a variety of formatting techniques. The publication is made from eight sheets of paper accordion-folded into 32-page sections and sewn into a book block. The book block is without a cover so that the stitching is exposed and becomes a feature of the design, rather than being hidden away, as it usually is.

The outer fold on each page is perforated, enabling readers to tear pages open (pages can be seen on page 131 of this book) to reveal the complete pagination. The gradual tearing that this process requires leaves the book increasingly ragged on the outer edge. Each copy of the publication thereby bears the marks of individual readers and their use of it.

Japanese binding

Japanese or stab binding is a binding method whereby the pages are sewn together with one continual thread. Pages do not open flat with this binding. This is a very decorative binding method, which is not commonly used but is very luxurious.

By its nature, this type of binding instills a sense of craft and attention to detail, as well as a sense of the handmade, as opposed to the formality of a mechanical process.

This brochure (left) for **Onitsuka Tiger** clothing company by **Eg.G** uses a Japanese binding to provide a decorative element to the flock cover, both elements thereby reflecting the clothing trade that the client is involved in.

This technique is further described in the DIY Binding section of this book, on page 165.

Loose-leaf binding
Along with traditional approaches to binding, there are many more informal ones. These include innovative approaches, as shown here and on page 160, where an elastic band is used to 'bind' loose-leaf items. This example (right) by **Thirteen** for photographer **Peter Thorpe** uses two greyboards and elastic bands to bind the photographer's samples. Once opened, the recipient can choose to order and juxtapose the images as they wish.

A binding method is generally selected for the functional purpose it serves, and in this book, **'Hours'**, by **Struktur**, the use of two books makes a physical separation in the work. Half the book is a calendar of hours while the other half comprises paintings by an artist created within a certain amount of time. Each part is produced as a separate book of loose-leaf pages, informally bound with an elastic band, perhaps suggesting the elasticity of time.

DIY Binding#1

Simple thread sewn example
The following example is a simple thread-sewn binding, similar to the standard, utilitarian saddle stitch (stapled) binding we are familiar with, but offering more room for experimentation.

1 Folding

Folding paper appears simple, but it is actually harder then you would imagine to do it correctly. Firstly, ensure you have a clean flat surface to work on, and a folding 'bone' to score, create and fold paper with.

Secondly, paper has a grain. You should always fold with the grain, and not against it. The grain is created by the fibres of the paper laying in a certain way, and papers can be described as short or long grain depending on the way the fibres lie.

To establish grain direction (this is easier and more obvious in heavier papers), tear a sheet across both directions. One should tear in a straighter line, with the grain, while the other, working against the grain will be more jagged.

Alternatively, you can bend the paper. The bend with least resistance is parallel to the grain.

2 Measuring and punching

Carefully measure out the distance of holes for the binding on to a template sheet. Using a bookbinding bradle and cradle, you can punch through the holes, a few sheets at a time from the template (don't try to do too many sheets in one go). A bookbinding cradle has a space for the bradle to pass through, creating clean and consistent holes.

3 Trim
Carefully guillotine the folded pages or use a sharp craft knife and metal edge ruler to create a neat cut.

The finished book binding has a sense of craft and these basic principles are the basis of many more elaborate designs, as the next example will demonstrate.

DIY Binding#2

Japanese thread sewn example
The following example is a Japanese thread sewn binding. Additional 'value' can be added by altering the colours and textures of materials and thread.

1 Collate pages

Collate the pages that you intend to bind; in this case the pages are a black stock. Apply a protective cover, front and back; in this case a sheet of white paper. Use a clothes peg to keep the pages together so they don't slip when drilling and threading.

A flat, clean surface is important to ensure the stock, especially if highly gloss or matt in nature, doesn't get marked or damaged.

2 Mark out drill-holes

Mark out the position of the drill-holes on to the white stock (which will later be discarded). This way, the book stock doesn't get marked or damaged. Holes are usually placed around 10 mm apart and 7–10 mm from the edge.

You can additionally 'pre-score' the pages with a vertical indent, allowing them to open more easily. This is useful if the stock is heavy and not very pliable.

3 Collate pages
Once marked out, the holes are ready to be drilled.

4c Drilling
Alternatively, carefully use a hand-held drill.

4a Drilling
Slowly drill the holes, ensuring the paper doesn't slip.

5 Peel back the protective sheet
This will allow access to binding.

4b Drilling
A fixed drill is best but it can be done with a bradle or awl if the pages are light.

6a Threading
Thread your needle with chosen cord.

6b Threading
Thread and bind the book, using the cover sheet to keep the outer stock clean.

7 Tie and cut
Do a final tie-off on the thread and carefully cut the cord. Now the white protective sheet and pegs that have been keeping the cover cloth clean can be removed.

The resulting pattern of thread can be altered, allowing for individuality and experimentation: these range from the very geometric (as in the example on this page) to more elaborate and free in nature. The colour of the thread can also be used to enhance a sense of continuity or branding, and can be single, dual or multi-coloured.

Pre-printed pages can be used to make personal portfolios, photographic books or short-run editions that have a sense of craft and invested time.

'What gunpowder did for war the printing press has done for the mind.'

Wendell Phillips

Chapter 6
Print and finish

Printing has played a fundamental role in our global development since its first incarnations as early as 3500 BCE, when clay 'documents' were created with cylinder seals by the Persian and Mesopotamian civilisations. Later, woodblock printing (now known as xylography) was developed, allowing multiple copies of documents to be printed; wood typefaces are still used today in letterpress printing. The limitations of wood (it is fragile and breaks), led to the development of Johannes Gutenberg's movable metal type printing in the mid-fifteenth century, from which all modern printing derives, and indeed his printing press design remained practically unchanged for 300 years.

Many finishing techniques were developed to protect printed items and to increase longevity but are now used more for creative effect and to instill a sense of identity into a design.

This final chapter looks at some of the creative approaches designers can adopt, using both traditional and contemporary print and finishing techniques.

Printing

Each printing technique, be it letterpress, lino or screen-printing has its own advantages (and limitations). The printing method selected will influence the design of a piece of communication, and will also carry certain connotations. Letterpress has a sense of nostalgia, lino a sense of craft and screen-printing a sense of the immediate and hand-produced.

Letterpress

Letterpress printing is a form of relief printing, traditionally using wood or metal blocks, composed into a 'chase', or 'bed', as shown top left. These characters are then printed, using a mechanical or hand press to leave an impression in the paper. You can also produce prints using a burnisher, as shown top right. The characterful nature of lots of the fonts cut and cast in letterpress is often exploited by designers (as in the case opposite), not least because as the characters are printed, over time they degrade and take on more and more imperfections. Letterpress has enjoyed a revival, perhaps in contrast to the proliferation of digital media, and many designers are developing and progressing this tradition, as in the case on the following spread.

Frost Design created a catalogue (opposite) without binding and without a cover for book imprint **4th Estate**. The heavyweight, loose-leaf cards have been letterpressed and are presented in a storage box. The stock choice provides greater durability, and allows for a deep impression from the letterpress printing process.

Pennsylvania-based letterpress studio **Gingerly Press** created these simultaneously natural yet magical compositions (above and opposite) from fragments collated on a hike of the Appalachian Trail (Georgia to Maine) in 2017. **The Printed Walk: Georgia to Maine**.

Each piece is a celebration of the small beauties discovered on the walk, including some scavenged textures, like fallen birch bark and pigments of charcoal caused by wildfires, that were later used in the delicate printed pieces. Combined with metal and wood type and carved plywood blocks, the compositions are an eclectic mix of strong compositional form, and exemplify the subtle beauty of letterpress printing.

Lino

Lino printing uses sheets of linoleum that are cut into using shaped blades (below) to create an image in reverse, which is then printed on to paper using a printing press or roller. Invented by Frederick Walton around 1860, this process has gone on to be adopted by designers and artists including the constructivists who exploited its inherent simplicity. In contrast to letterpress, that gives texture to a print, lino is totally flat and gives an even reliable print. Generally, these designs were produced in black on white, exploiting the contrast of the colours, however, lino can be used with a range of materials and printing colours.

Multiple coloured prints can be created with careful planning, creating ever more elaborate designs and allowing for the overprinting of inks, adding texture and interest to a design. Linocutting, by its nature is time-consuming, but ultimately produces a tactile and engaging design.

Designers **Webb & Webb** make creative use of lino in this book series (opposite) for publisher and printer, **Hand & Eye Letterpress**. Chris Brown's illustrations bring Holly Skeet's story to life in a series of playful linocuts. The standard edition of the book is printed on one-colour lino, with a special edition of the book, pictured opposite, available with additional 'colouring-in' from the artist.

PAW PRINTS

A Story by Holly Skeet

Pictures by Chris Brown

Hand & Eye Editions

Sure enough, a few weeks of puzzling over the circus handbills had paid off. Joshua's vocabulary was rather heavy on adjectives such as *death-defying* and *world-famous*, but he could read. And he was the proud owner of a book. It had been left behind by a small girl in a sticky dress, and Joshua had appropriated it. It was called *A Treasury of Fantastic Beasts*. The dramatic illustrations showed strange creatures from other lands such as the *Biscuity Penguin* and the *Giraffe* **Grotesque**.

Joshua's favourite chapter was about a six-foot bull-terrier who had menaced a small principality. Some days, when the circus cats had been more unspeakably rude than usual, he wondered what had happened to that dog. Of course, by the end of his career Joshua had acquired several other books, but the *Treasury* was always the one he liked best. He liked to think that, he, Joshua T. Barker, could have been a *Fantastic Beast* himself.

Screen-printing

Screen-printing is a technique where a mesh screen (originally made from silk) is used in conjunction with a squeegee to push ink (which has been mixed with a medium) through to a substrate, except in the areas that have been 'blocked' off.

Screen-printing offers lots of experimentation and control over the way a design is printed. The 'size' of the screen affects the way a design looks, and screens range from very fine, affording great detail and complexity, to broader screens for coarser work and application on to fabric.

There are two main techniques for preparing a design and exposing a screen. Firstly, if you have access to the equipment, you can use photo-emulsion to block off areas that won't print, as shown below. This technique can also be simulated using sunlight to expose the screen. Alternatively, a low-tech version can be done simply using stencils or scraps of paper, as shown opposite.

This technique is also known as 'serigraphy' or 'serigraph' printing.

Shown opposite is a low-tech workshop run by **Gavin Ambrose and Beth Salter** using pre-cut paper stencils. The shapes can be overprinted, and, depending on the amount of medium added to the ink, allow varying degrees of 'showthrough'.

Print finishing

In addition to the different methods of folding and binding we have just explored, there also exists a range of print finishing techniques which can be used to enhance and enliven a piece of work. Often a piece of print will contain one or more additional items of print finishing: these can include engineering of paper stocks by bonding them together, known as duplexing, or using special inks and varnishes.

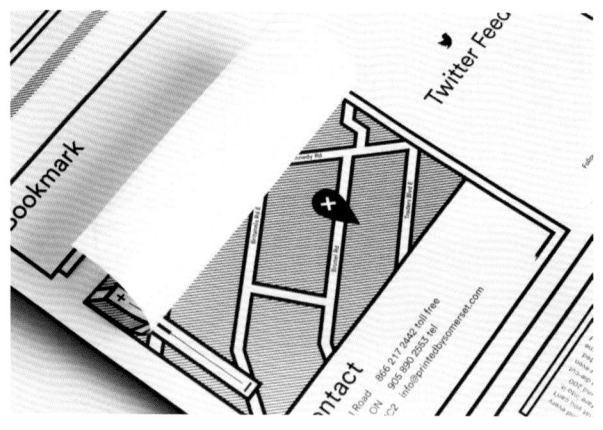

Sticker

Scanimation

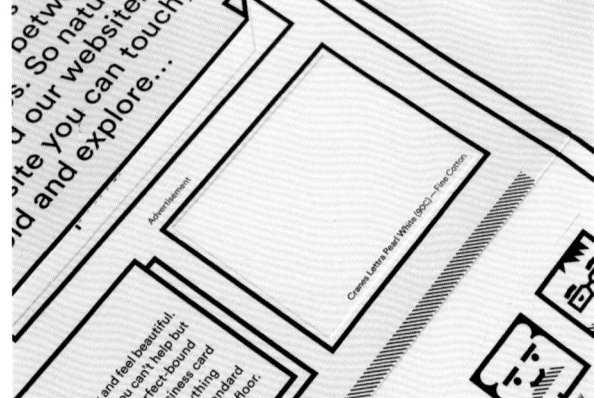

Tipped-on paper sample

Duplex (bonding of two paper stocks)

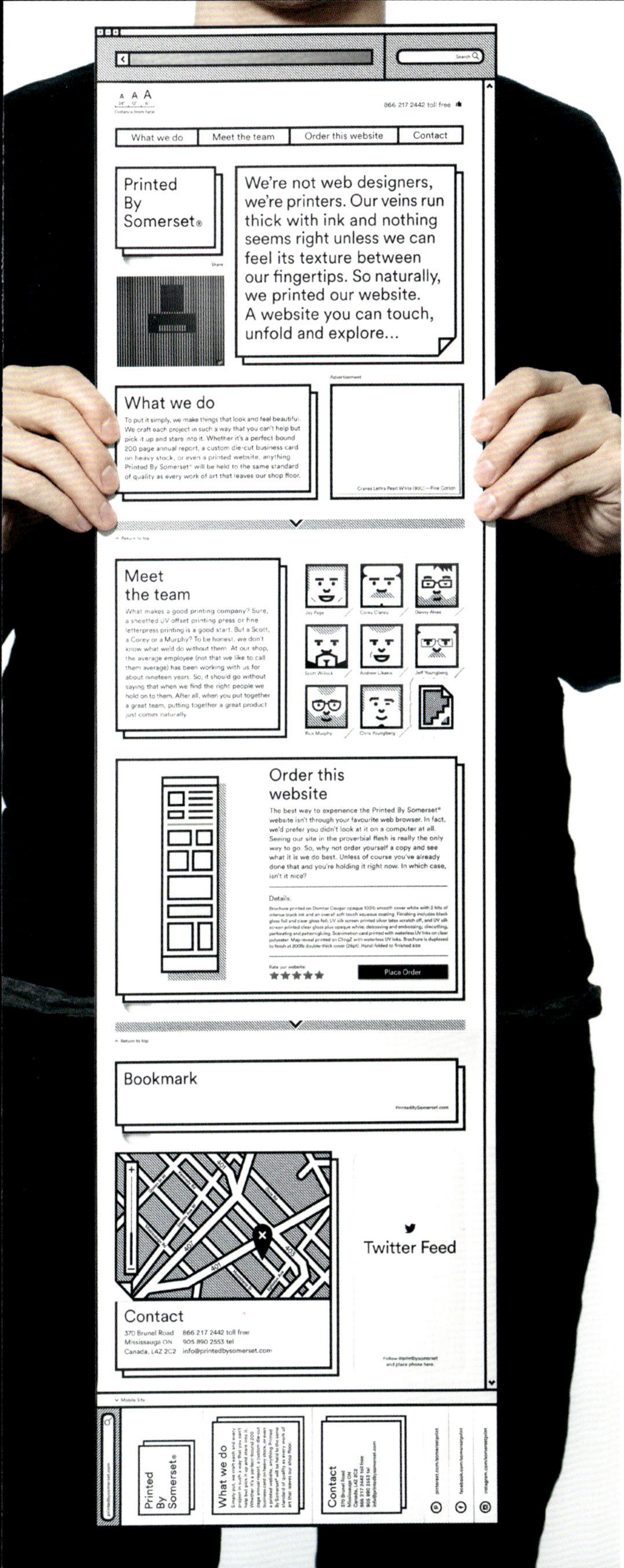

Toronto-based studio **Leo Burnett Worldwide** designed this mailer for one of Canada's most prominent printers, **Somerset**. **'Printed By Somerset'** is a mailer that reflects a new website focussed on print and detail. The piece contains a spectrum of print finishing to showcase the capabilities and possibilities of print as a medium.

Perforation

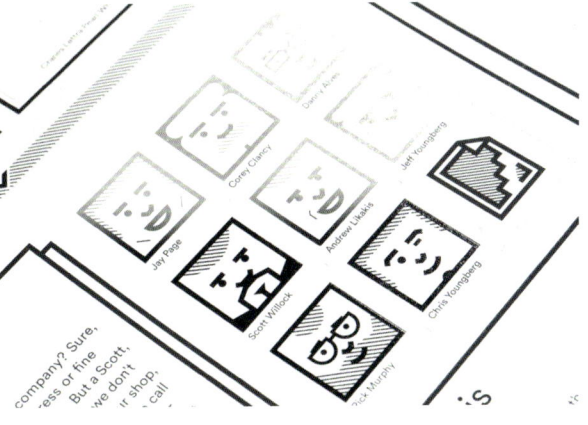

Clear foil detail

Filigree

A filigree is traditionally an ornamental work in which fine gold or silver wire is used to create intricate patterns.

This cover for **The Rolling Stones** Bridges to Babylon CD (left), designed by **Stefan Sagmeister** and **Hjalti Karlsson**, featured an illustration of an Assyrian lion by **Kevin Murphy**. The illustration is emphasised by a special filigree slipcase that outlines the lion with an intricate arabesque detail.

Embossing and debossing

An emboss is a design stamped into a substrate without ink or foil, resulting in a raised surface. When a stamp is used to give a recessed surface, the process is called debossing. The two processes are used to give decorative, textured effects to a publication and are typically used to provide emphasis to certain elements of the design.

With the marketing of real estate, taking ownership of an address has distinct advantages. Potential buyers begin to see a building as an important part of an already important street, and this sales brochure for a new building at **30 Gresham Street**, London (opposite), designed by **Hat-trick**, does just that – by employing the use of the number 30 throughout. The lid has 30 words representing the values of the development embossed on it, and the box contains two half-sized brochures with '30' foil-blocked on the covers. One brochure contains 30 words and the other contains 30 images. A series of guides of the neighbouring vicinity covers '30 points of view', '30 minutes around Gresham Street', '30 illustrious neighbours' and a map with '30 ways to Gresham Street'.

Die cut

Die cutting is a process that uses a steel die to cut away a section of a page. Die cuts have many uses and are mainly used for decorative purposes to enhance the visual performance of a design. However, they may also serve a physical function, such as by making unusual shapes or creating apertures that allow users to see inside a publication.

Die cuts create graphic forms as they reveal content behind, as in the examples on this page (below and right) by **Studio Makgill** for paper manufacturer **G . F Smith**. The use of paper engineering and die cuts cleverly articulates the brand values of the paper manufacturer while appealing to the core market of designers and print buyers as they explore the paper stocks in a very immediate and tactile way.

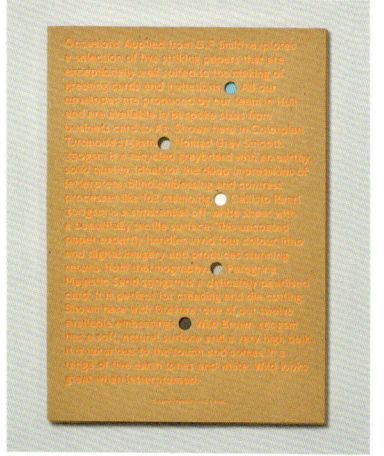

Colour, typographic style, paper stocks and shape can all significantly contribute to the successful creation of an identity and brand. For the **'Somewhere Totally Else'** exhibition at the **Design Museum** in London, **Studio Myerscough** created an invite with die-cut letterforms.

Hat-trick used the natural relationship between the letters 'r' and 'h' in their stationery design for interior design company **Rabih Hage**. The 'r' is die cut out of the 'h', and provides a 'window' into the interior content. Shown here (left) is a folded business card from the range.

Format for Graphic Designers

Laser etching

Laser etching or laser cutting an artwork is similar to die cutting, but it allows a thicker substrate to be cut through. In addition to cutting all the way through a material, a laser cutter can also be finely controlled to etch into the surface of a material. The laser can be set to go into the substrate by a very accurate measurement, allowing delicate control over how pronounced the 'burn' is. With some substrates, as in the **G . F Smith** stock shown below, this creates the illusion of an emboss. In other substrates such as timber (right), this creates more of a burnt effect and includes a dusting 'haloing' effect.

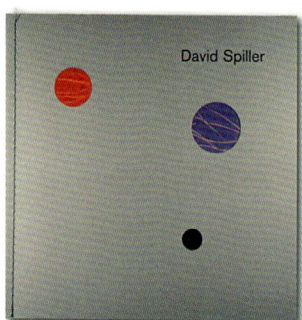

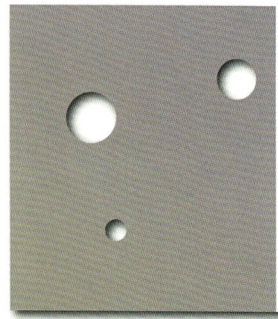

Creative destruction in design can produce both striking and effective results, as this business card (above) by **The Kitchen** where a laser was used to burn a pattern of holes into the substrate, illustrates. On a white stock such as this, the laser creates small burn rings around each hole. These burn rings can be hidden by overprinting with a solid colour, but in this case, creative director Rob Petrie intentionally left them visible. The burn marks appear on the back of the card, as seen on the left of the photograph opposite. The soft textured blue hues create a soft backdrop for the strong graphic intervention.

For a collection of David Spiller paintings for **Beaux Arts** that all featured circles, **Studio AS** used a die cut to hint at what lies within the catalogue's pages, rather than simply relying on an image (left).

Kiss cut
Kiss cut is a method of die cutting whereby the face material of a self-adhesive substrate is die cut but not right through to the backing sheet. This enables the face material to be easily removed from the backing sheet. For the cover of a brochure (below) for **NESTA** – the UK's National Endowment for Science, Technology and the Arts – **Hat-trick** used a self-adhesive substrate kiss cut into stickers, inviting readers to distribute the 'subject to change' message they carry.

Perforation
A perforation is a series of cuts or holes manufactured on a form to weaken paper for tearing. There are two main types of perforation: 'press perforation' or 'machine perforation', which is a method of inserting a sharp perforating ruler at the time of printing (or after at a specialist finishing house). For more low-tech perforating, a simple 'wheel perforation' can be used and these are readily available in craft shops.

A perforation allows a design to be paced in the way it reveals a narrative or information. It also adds a tactile interactive quality to a design, as in the work by **Studio Makgill** for **G . F Smith** shown on this page, where perforation serves as function, as in the tear of swatches below. It can also have a more playful nature, as shown opposite.

We proudly invite you to celebrate
the launch of Gmund Applied
on Thursday 17 March 2016
from 6.30pm until 10pm
at Bierschenke, 4 London Wall Buildings
Blomfield Street, London EC2M 5NT

RSVP by 9 March to
londonlaunch@gfsmith.com

We will be live letterpressing on
the night, so please bring this invite
with you to be turned into an
original artwork

Gmund Cotton New Grey 110gsm with
Gmund Cotton Power Blue 900gsm from G.F Smith

Chapter 6 / Print and finish

Fore-edge printing
Fore-edge printing was traditionally done as a way of protecting the fore-edge of a book. This is commonly seen in bibles and other large volumes where the paper is especially thin.

It has now been adopted for more visual and tactile purposes. In the example by **SAS**, (right), a sculptural quality is instilled by printing the edges of the book in black. The book, a self-promotional piece for the design practice, documents the working reality of the studio and the thin fluorescent bookmark mounted on the front features statistical information that relates to the formation of the company.

The page opposite shows an example of printing on to the open bind of a book, creating a tactile and engaging title for the degree show catalogue for the University of Brighton Graphic Design and Illustration BA (Hons) course show titled **Studio 350**. This catalogue features an open spine and a tipped-on image on the front cover, with the only text appearing printed on the exposed outer spine.

193

Chapter 6 / Print and finish

Lamination and spot UV
Spot varnishing is the application of varnish to a specific area of a printed piece, usually providing full coverage of an image. In-line or 'wet' varnishing as a fifth or sixth colour during printing adds a wet layer of varnish on to a wet layer of ink. As they dry, they absorb into the stock together, which diminishes the impact. Off-line varnishing applies the varnish as a separate pass once the inks have dried, and results in extra glossiness, as less is absorbed by the stock. A UV spot varnish is a high-gloss varnish applied to selected areas of a design, to enhance, impact or form part of the graphic design that results in a raised texture.

This design by **NB Studio**, for the **Crafts Council**, features a heavily laminated cover-board that is folded back on itself and glued. Two vertical parallel creases form a sculptural and rigid spine.

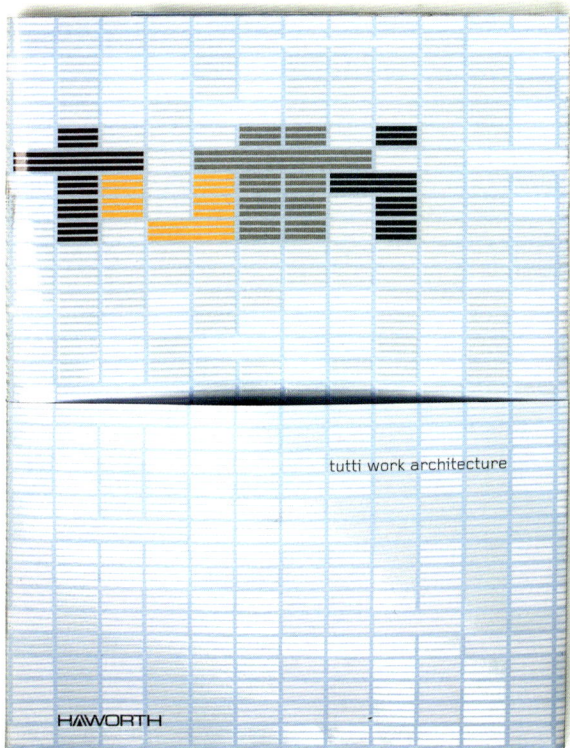

This design for **tutti work architecture** by **North** is a poster-wrapped publication that contains a number of throws and a three-panel gatefold back cover. The brochure explores how changes to the physical work environment can alter and foster a more productive working culture in an organisation. The bar design appears throughout the publication, sometimes as a graphic and other times as a more subtle spot varnish.

Foil
Also known as a hot foil stamp, this process uses heat to transfer metallic foil to a substrate. Foils range from flat colours to holographic patterns and add a tactile element to a design. The reflective qualities of a foil vary from matt, flat colours through to reflective metallics and even holographic effects.

Shown left is the cover for *The Shopmodern Condition* by Swedish design theorist and critic Linda Rampell for **Art And Theory Publishing**. The book's content, exploring consumerism and 'worth', is clearly articulated in this design by **Gabor Palotai** using a simple graphic foil.

To mark the fiftieth anniversary of the death of Frank Lloyd Wright, **Clarke & Reilly** curated and hosted an exhibition of works inspired by the architect at their London showroom. The invites (opposite), by **Morse Design**, use a matt, red foil square (a reference to the mark that adorned Wright's drawings), stamped on a thick greyboard. Finer, typographic details are stamped in black foil, creating a strong typographic identity.

CLARKE & REILLY PRESENTS FRANK. AN EXHIBITION
OF WORK BY 6 ARTISTS CRAFTSPEOPLE INSPIRED
BY THE DESIGNS OF FRANK LLOYD WRIGHT. CURATED
BY BRIDGET DWYER AND DAVID GROCOTT.
FEATURING WORK BY MARY DWYER PAINTINGS/
JAMES PLUMB LIGHTING/CLARA VULETICH WALLPAPER/
MARTIN TUCKER FURNITURE/LUCY GRIFFITHS TEXTILES/
KIRSTEN HECKTERMANN TEXTILES
EXHIBITION RUNS 22 OCTOBER—19 NOVEMBER 2009
PRIVATE VIEW WEDNESDAY 21 OCTOBER 6.30PM—9PM
C&R

8 PORCHESTER PLACE, LONDON
+44 (0)20 7262 3500 / INFO@CLARKEANDR
WWW.CLARKEANDREILLY.COM
C&R

Flock

Flock is a very fine woollen refuse or vegetable fibre dust that is used to coat paper. It is fixed with an adhesive to give the substrate a velvety or cloth-like appearance. The process of flocking can be traced back to around 1000 BCE China, where glues were used to bond fibres to fabrics for wall coverings. This was popularised during the Middle Ages in Europe and celebrated in the opulence of Louis XIV's reign in France.

Paper manufacturers and designers have adopted the flocking process for printing substrates to give a textural, human addition to the printing process.

It is possible to print on to flock, but the results vary as it isn't a consistent material. Consequently, a foil stamp is often used to apply text and basic shapes instead of standard ink.

'Dolly' is an alternative typeface catalogue for a new typeface called 'Dolly', designed by **Underware**. Dolly is also the name of the canine character who features in the product's logo, which is foil-blocked on to the cover of the catalogue designed by **Faydherbe De Vringer**.

Tip-ins

A tip-in is a means to attach an insert into a book or magazine by gluing along the binding edge. Traditionally, it is a method for attaching individual elements into a publication (such as colour plates) that are typically produced on a different stock and where insufficient pages are required to warrant printing a separate section. However, the tip-in has been adopted by contemporary designers as a means of adding interest and a sense of reveal to a publication. If the tipped-in pages are shorter or narrower than the main book, they can mask certain areas of the page behind, and reveal others. Tip-ins can be used to mask images (above), to create juxtapositions of images (opposite top), or clearly divide pages (opposite bottom).

In books that are perfect bound, the tip-in can go in between any of the pages. In contrast, a book that is Coptic bound or saddle stitched will require more planning, as the tip-in has to nestle in between pages and also has to come out on the other side of the section to be secure.

Shown on these pages is *People Make Places Make People*, a book celebrating the twelve-year anniversary of architecture practice **Metropolitan Workshop**. The book features a series of interviews with staff, clients and contributors, as well as a history of the practice. The book is designed by **Studio245** and uses a complex series of tipped-in pages, creating a layered, archival feel.

Portrait Photography by Taran Wilkhu.

Chapter 6 / Print and finish

North used seven stocks to produce a mélange of textures for this brochure celebrating ten years of property developer **Manhattan Loft Corporation**. The design is based around colour plates set in white frames, each of which contain commissioned photography of the area. The frames are separated by translucent tip-ins, while undersized tip-ins of a heavier stock are used to provide additional reference information and atmospheric imagery. All the tip-ins bind from the same edge of the book (the bottom in this case) – a usual requirement when collating and binding.

This wiro-bound brochure by **HGV Felton** for **Esprit Europe** has five A4 leaves with 12 short varnished tip-ins between heavy uncoated cover stock. The imagery of the tipped-in elements is based on the Solari analogue information display system common in airports and train stations to convey messages. The rich, atmospheric black and white imagery draws attention to the spine of the publication where the wiro binding is used as the hinge in the message system that readers are invited to interact with.

Glossary

Accordion or concertina fold
Two or more parallel folds that go in opposite directions and open out like an accordion.

A series paper sizes
ISO metric standard paper size based on the square root of two ratio. The A0 sheet (841mm x 1189mm) is one square metre and each size (A1, A2, A3, A4 etc.) has a ratio of height divided by the width of square root of two (1.4142).

Basis weight
The weight, measured in pounds, of 500 sheets (a ream) of paper cut to a standard size.

Bellyband
A printed band that wraps around a publication; typically used with magazines.

Bible paper or India paper
A thin, lightweight, long-life, opaque paper grade typically made from 25% cotton and linen rags or flax with chemical wood pulp, named after its most common usage.

Bleed printing
When the printed information extends past where the page will be trimmed so that the colours or images continue to the edge of the cut page.

Brittleness
Meaning easily broken, an important paper attribute to be aware of when considering folding as you do not want it to crack.

B series paper sizes
ISO metric standard paper size based on the square root of two ratio. B sizes are intermediate sizes to the A series sizes.

Buckram
A coarse linen or cotton fabric sized with glue or gum, used for covering a hardcover binding.

Burst binding
At the folding stage the sections are perforated on the binding side to allow glue to penetrate into each fold of paper. The glued spine then has a cover applied and wrapped around the book block.

Canadian binding
A spiral-bound volume with a wraparound cover that can stand up better on a shelf, with a spine for the title. Half-Canadian has an exposed spiral, a full Canadian does' not.

Case or edition binding
A common hardcover bookbinding method that sews signatures together, flattens the spine, applies end sheets and head and tail bands to the spine.

Concertina fold
See Accordion fold.

Crack-back
A backing stock with a self-adhesive coating that may have a die cut to make it easier to peel away from the stock it backs.

Creasing
A process using a blade and pressure to impart a crease into a substrate so that it can subsequently be folded. Similar to a die cut except the blade does not penetrate the substrate.

Creep
Creep occurs in a saddle-stitched publication when the bulk of the paper causes the inner pages to extend (creep) further than the outer pages when folded.

Cross fold
Two or more folds going in different directions, typically at right angles. Mainly used in book work where paper is cross folded and cut to form a signature.

Deboss
As emboss but recessed into the substrate.

Deckle or feather edge
This is the ragged edge of the paper as it comes from the paper-making machine. Machine-made paper has two deckle edges, handmade has four. When not cut off it can serve a decorative purpose. An imitation deckle edge can be created by tearing the edge of the paper.

Die cut
Special shapes cut in a substrate by a steel die.

Double gatefold
Three panels that fold into the middle of a publication. These are slightly smaller in width to the inner panels so that when folded they nest inside the publication.

Duotone
A duotone is a two-colour reproduction from a monochrome original.

Dust jacket
A jacket around a hardback publication that originally offered protection against dirt and dust, as the name suggests, but more recently has become an integral graphic extension of the book and a key device for promotion.

Emboss
A design stamped without ink or foil giving a raised surface.

Endpaper or end sheets
The heavy cartridge paper pages at the front and back of a hardback book that join the book block to the hardback binding. Sometimes feature maps, a decorative colour or design.

Extent
Number of pages in a book.

Fan fold
A fan fold or accordion fold is a series of parallel folds made in the opposite direction to the previous fold along its length and then one right-angle fold to create a fan.

Flock
A speciality cover paper produced by coating the sheet with adhesive in patterns or all over, after which a dyed flock powder is applied. Originally intended to simulate tapestry and Italian velvet brocade.

Flood colour
A term referring to the colour fill of an item.

Foil, heat or hot stamp
Foil pressed on to a substrate using heat and pressure. Also known as block print or foil emboss.

Folio or page
A sheet of paper folded in half is a folio and each half of the folio is one page. A single folio has four pages.

French fold
A sheet of paper that is only printed on one side and folded with two right-angle folds to form a four-page, uncut section. The section is sewn through the fold while the top edges remain folded and untrimmed.

Frontispiece
An illustration inserted to face the title page.

Gatefold
The left and right edges fold inward with parallel folds and meet in the middle of the page without overlapping.

Grain
Paper grain is the direction in which most of its fibres lay and is determined during the papermaking process. The grain flows in the direction that the paper passes through the paper-making machine.

Imposition
The arrangement of pages in the sequence and position they will appear when printed before being cut, folded and trimmed.

International Paper Sizes (ISO)
A range of standard metric paper sizes.

Japanese or stab binding
A binding method whereby the pages are sewn together with one continual thread.

Kiss cut
A method of die cutting whereby the face material of a self-adhesive substrate is die cut but not completely through to the backing sheet. This enables the face material to be easily removed from the backing sheet.

Laminate
A laminate is a stock made by bonding two or more layers of stock together. Typically used to provide a thick cover stock comprising a cheap inner with a printable outer.

Loose-leaf binding
A binding method in which individual, punched sheets are loosely held by a binder.

Litho
A printing technique in which the ink is transferred from a printing plate to a 'blanket' cylinder and then to the paper or material on which it is to be printed.

Perforation
A series of cuts or holes manufactured on a form to weaken it for tearing.

Ream
500 sheets of paper.

Recto/Verso
The pages of an open book with recto being the right-hand page and verso the left-hand.

Saddle-stitching
A binding method used for booklets, programmes and small catalogues. Signatures are nested and wire stitches are applied through the spine along the centrefold. When opened, saddle-stitched books lay flat.

Showthrough or strikethrough
Where printing inks can be seen through the substrate on the reverse of the page. Particularly common with thin paper stocks and/or those with low loadings of fillers and coating; it is generally undesirable.

Side-stitching
A binding method for publications that are too bulky for saddle-stitching. Signatures are collated, placed flat under the stitching head and stapled. Side-stitched items do not lay flat when open.

Signature or section
A signature or section is a sheet of paper folded to form several pages which are collected together.

Slipcase
A protective case for a book or set of books open at one end so that only the book spines are visible.

Stock
Paper to be printed upon.

Substrate
The material or surface to be printed upon.

Tip-in
To attach an insert in a book or magazine by gluing along the binding edge such as to tip-in a colour plate.

UV coating
Coating applied to a printed substrate that is bonded and cured with ultraviolet light.

Varnish
A clear or tinted liquid shellac or plastic coating put on a printed piece to add a glossy, satin or dull finish applied like a final ink layer after a piece is printed (see front cover).

Vellum
Vellum is commonly used to mean a translucent paper although it can also mean a slightly rough paper finish.

Wiro/comb binding
A spine of plastic or wire rings that binds a document and allows it to open flat.

Z-bind
A 'z' shaped cover that is used to join two separate publications.

Index

3D shapes 44–7

accordion (concertina) fold
    examples 36, 143, 157, 204
    techniques 114–17, 120, 122–9, 130
adaptability over different platforms 52–6
adding value 14, 17, 19, 68–9, 152, 165
animation 110–11
ANSI paper sizes 74
apertures (punch-throughs/reveals) 38–9, 87–9, 184
'A' series paper sizes 74, 204

back/front folder 121
bags 20–2
basis weight 204
bellybands 138, 204
Bible paper 204
binding 144–69
    DIY thread sewn 161–9
    formal 152–3
    informal 154–9
    types 148–59
    uses of word 144
bleed printing 28, 31, 81, 115, 204
bones, folding paper 114, 118–19, 162
book marks 90, 192
boxes 16–19
bradle, hole punching 163, 167
brands/branding 24, 26–7, 48, 56–63, 185
'B' series paper sizes 204
buckram 16, 147, 149, 204
burnt paper 139, 187–8
burst binding 204

Canadian binding 153, 204
case (edition) binding 148, 204

collating pages 166
collectability 14, 17, 68–9
colour
    altered colour fall 80–1
    flood colour printing 28–9, 81, 145–60
    printing systems 43, 64
    varnish 80, 194
comb binding see wiro binding
commercial binding 146–53
communication 9, 12, 30, 33, 34, 43
    see also narrative
concertina fold see accordion fold
consistency over brand 56, 61
containment 12–26, 37
context 32–69
converging formats 52–5
covers
    dust jackets 148, 204
    multiple 68
    poster wraps 106–7, 195
    unusual materials 84–5, 198–9
    unusual shapes 41, 86–9, 138, 141, 194
    see also binding
crack-back 204
craft 9, 45, 113, 144, 145, 154, 158, 161–9, 172
creasing 194, 204
creep 114, 126, 204
cross fold 75, 204
'C' series envelope sizes 76

debossing 19, 182–3, 204
deckle edge 130–1, 204
die cutting
    apertures 38–9, 87, 88–9, 184–6, 188
    covers 126–7
    kiss cutting 189
    shaped publications 3,

7, 36, 46, 140
    techniques 184–6
dimensionality 46
double gatefold 120, 204
drilling holes, hand-binding 166–7
duelling z-fold 120
duotone 3, 204
duplexing 180
dust jackets 148, 204
    see also poster wraps

edition binding 148
elastic bands 36, 110–11, 159, 160
embossing 78, 124–5, 136, 182–3, 204
endorse folds 139
endpapers 147, 148, 204
envelopes 36, 73, 76–7
environmental impacts 64–5
extent of book 6, 204

fan fold 114–15, 205
filigree 182
film 50
finishing 180–203
flock 78, 85, 158, 198–9, 205
flood colour printing 28–9, 81, 145–60
foil stamping/blocking 19, 137, 181, 182–3, 196–7, 198, 205
folding 112–43, 162
folding bones 114, 118–19, 162
fold-outs 132
folio 72, 205
fonts 8, 30, 66–7, 172
fore-edge printing 192
formal bindings 152–3
form and function 34–43
form and shape 44–7
French folds 39, 130–1, 157, 205
front/back gatefold 120

frontispiece 205
full bleed 28, 31, 81

gatefolds 117, 120, 132–5, 195, 205
global contexts 33
grain of paper 162, 205
'graphic design', origin of term 40
grid designs 28, 100
guidelines, brands 56–63

half-Canadian binding 153
half cover from behind 120
hand binding 144, 158, 161–9
happy accidents 43, 64–5, 104
'haptic' approach 43
harmonica fold 126
history as inspiration 66
history of printing 171
holes
    hand binding 163, 166–7
    see also apertures

identity
    folding 140–1
    see also brands
imposition 80–1, 205
India paper 204
informal bindings 154–9
in-line varnishing 194
interactivity 13, 24, 38, 43, 50, 102–3, 190
International (ISO) paper sizes 74, 205

Japanese (stab) binding 158, 165–9, 205

kiss cutting 189

lamination 152, 194, 205
laser etching 187–8
layflat bindings 148, 149, 152–3

letterpress printing 172–5
letterpress typography 9, 66–7
lino printing 176–7
lithographic (litho) printing 64, 205
loose-leaf binding 16, 86, 159–60, 172–3, 205

magazines 68, 98–101, 132–3
mailers 36, 143
maquettes (printer's dummies) 114–15, 123, 145, 150
measuring paper 114, 163
mock book fold 120
mountain and valley folds 118–19, 128
multiple covers 68
multiple stocks 80–3, 202

narrative 10–31
    created by users 43
    revealed 12–13, 38–9, 106–7, 116, 190, 195
    storytelling 28–31
newspapers and newspaper format 94–7
newsprint paper 75, 78
nostalgia 66, 172

octavo paper 72
off-line varnishing 194
online media 48–50, 94
open binding 154–7, 192–3
order in design 40–1

packaging 12, 14–19, 24–7, 45, 69
page marker ribbons 91
paper
    burning 139, 187–8
    folding 112–43
    grain 162
    sizes 72–4, 94
    stocks 78–83, 184, 202, 205
patternicity 28
perfect binding 148, 149, 200
perforations
    French folded pages 39, 130, 157
    mailers 73
    tear off sections 102–3, 110, 143, 181, 190
    techniques 190–1, 205
    z-binds 150, 151
photo-emulsion screen printing 178
planning, book printing 80–1
posters 102–9, 128
poster wraps 106–7, 195
printed media 70–111
printer's dummies (maquettes) 114–15, 123, 145, 150
print finishing 180–203
printing 171–9
protection 6, 11, 12, 14, 16, 24, 142, 148, 152
prototypes 44, 145
    see also maquettes
punching holes 163, 167
punch-throughs see apertures
purpose of design 10–31

quarto paper 72

randomness 42–3
reader's ribbons 91
ream of paper 205
recto/verso pages 205
revealing the narrative 12–13, 38–9, 106–7, 116, 190, 195
reveals see apertures
risograph duplicator 64–5
roll fold 117
rubber (elastic) bands 36, 110–11, 159, 160

saddle-stitching 148, 200, 205
scale/size of publication 72–3, 92–3, 98–9
screen-printing 178–9
sculptural forms 84–91
self-covers 117, 120, 123–7, 142–3, 147
serigraphy/serigraph printing 178–9
shape and form 44–7

short print runs 44, 64, 94
show-through (strike-through) 130, 178, 205
side stitching 205
    see also Japanese binding
signatures (sections) 148, 205
silk-screen printing 178–9
size see scale; standard paper sizes
slipcases 14–15, 182, 205
small-scale manufacture 8, 44
special editions 68, 99, 132, 176–7
spines of books 146, 148, 153, 154–6, 192–4
spot UV 64, 194
spot varnishing 36, 80, 194, 195
stab binding see Japanese binding
standard paper sizes 72–4, 94
staples 148
stencil screen printing 178–9
stickers 180, 189
stocks (paper types) 78–83, 184, 202, 205
storytelling see narrative
substrates 76, 79, 84, 138, 152, 182, 187–9, 198, 205
    see also stocks
sustainability 64–5

throw-outs, folded pages 132–7
throw-ups, folded pages 136–7
tip-ins 200–3, 205
transparent/translucent paper 34–5, 202
trimming hand-bound books 164
triple parallel fold 120
typefaces 20, 25
typography 8, 9, 30–1, 61–3, 66–7, 172

US paper sizes 74
UV coating 194, 205

valley and mountain folds 118–19, 128
value, adding value 14, 17, 19, 68–9, 152, 165
values, of brands 56, 130
varnishing 36, 80, 194, 195, 203, 205
vellum 205

wiro (comb) binding 152, 203, 205
wooden objects 44–5
wooden printing blocks 171–2
wrap folders/covers 40, 86, 138, 143
    see also bellybands; poster wraps; self covers

z-binds 150–1, 205
z-folds 120, 140, 151

Acknowledgements

We would like to thank everyone who supported us during the project including the many art directors, designers and creatives who showed great generosity in allowing us to reproduce their work. Special thanks to everyone that hunted for, collated, compiled and rediscovered some of the fascinating work contained in this book. Thanks to Xavier Young for his patience, determination and skill in photographing the work showcased in this book, and to Heather Marshall for modelling. Big thanks to Leafy Cummins for all her patient editing and all the staff at Bloomsbury Publishing who never tired of our requests, enquiries and questions, and supported us throughout.

A huge thank you to Chloe Legret for her work on picture research and for designing and photographing the breaker pages. Thank you to Katie Fitzgibbon and Ella Simmonds for doing the photo shoots of workshops on pages 114, 117, 118, 119, 121, 122, 126, 146, 160–169, and 176.

And a final big thank you to Lindsay Schmittle at Gingerly Press for allowing me to reuse her fabulous work on the cover of this book.

Picture credits

Page 19: Designed by John Morgan Studio with David Chipperfield Architects
Page 67: Richard Ardagh and Adrian Harrison
Page 105: Neo Neo: Thuy-An Hoang, Xavier Erni
Page 129 and 157: Design by Melanie Crolla at Born © BORN DESIGN LIMITED
Page 174 and 175: Copyright 2018 Gingerly Press. Portrait photo by Nicole Young, Girl Photography
Page 184, 190 and 191: Design by Studio Makgill, photographs by Peter Guenzel
Page 196: Gabor Palotai Design: Linda Rampell – The Shopmodern Condition, Book design
Page 201: Portrait photography by Taran Wikhu.